T5-AES-362

THE SPECTATOR'S guide to SOCCER

Published in United States of America by
Soccer Publishing, Inc.; PO Box 1417; Princeton, NJ 08542.

ISBN: 0-935644-09-1
Library of Congress Card Catalog Number: 89-064337

Cover Design by Miho Kahn.
Diagrams by Breedon Books, Derby, England.
Printed in the United States of America.

CONTENTS

Introduction

FIFTEEN-plus years ago when my kids began playing soccer, I was one among a throng of dutiful parents who were standing along the sidelines, shuffling our feet, smiling vaguely, avoiding eye contact, limiting our conversations to the likelihood of rain, and being especially careful only to applaud when others did . . .all to avoid divulging our ignorance of what we were watching.

"I don't know about the rest of you, but I feel like an idiot not having the foggiest idea what's going on out there!"

Eventually someone would break down and confess what we all felt, bringing a glad-you-admitted-it-first chorus of agreement that what we needed was a quick-and-easy guide for soccer spectators.

I never figured I would be the one to write such a guide, but fate does take strange turns that have their own unique logic.

Since more kids (and then their parents) wanted to play than there were knowledgeable "soccerists" to guide them, I was chucked into the coaching cauldron. From the comfortable world of Little League, where any American male adult was assumed to be savant, I now was on the same level with my players, and had to prove my right to tell them what to do, which meant finding out for myself first . . .a distinctly humbling experience!

More than 500 games later, coaching boys and girls, men and women, from the world's near-best to the world's near-worst and everything in between, I'm still at it, and probably will be, when they have to wheel me out there and prop me up. Maybe this bespeaks stubbornness more than common sense, but the experience is ideal for my purposes here.

Naturally, from the beginning I sought guidance from people to whom soccer was as natural as football, baseball and basketball is to us. Luckily, in the Washington, D.C. area there were plenty such people, and I appreciate their willing contributions even if I can reference only a few by name.

Of course, my first steps were to seek *written* guidance via soccer coaching manuals. Since all were (and still are) written by guys *brought up* with soccer in other lands, they assume you know what "football" is all about, and that you're thirsting for details of its evolution, the origins and nuances of formations, and player development.

And when they finally do get around to what you came for — *how soccer is actually played* — they barrage you with diagrams that would baffle the most advanced computers. (Let's see now, do the dashes mean passes or are those the squiggly lines? And how come player #7 seems to be in *five* places at the same time?)

For us, the hardest aspect to grasp is that soccer players are interchangeable units who can be anywhere at any time without pause or apparent reason. #7, like everyone else, is free to roam where he or she chooses, and the trend in international soccer is towards even more unfettered movement. I'll try to clarify aspects like this as we progress.

I've pored through these manuals, because I've *had* to, but they're heavy stuff for people who *don't* have to . . .for those who just want to know enough to enjoy what they see from the sidelines, the stands, or the couch. Perhaps soccer will especially be viewed from the couch, as it will be hitting the tube big-time in coming years.

So, my purpose is to provide basic viewer familiarity by explaining soccer, as I had to learn and teach it myself, in terms of our own more familiar sports.

As such, this is hardly the definitive work on the topic. (If I could write it, you wouldn't read it!) It's what the word "guide" implies, a handy reference that focuses on the essentials from two perspectives . . .what you see now, and what you will see later.

Although the United States has never been a factor in the international equation, this is changing. We are making serious and sometimes surprisingly successful efforts . . .especially and significantly with our youth teams. . .to challenge the rest of the world.

And, for the first time ever, the United States will host the World Cup final round in 1994.

The World Cup will certainly be the largest *sporting* event in our history. Throughout the latter part of 1993 and early 1994, more than 100 countries will vie for a place in the final 24. Those that make it . . .the U.S. as host gets an automatic spot . . .will play a total of 52 games (most of them televised) in ten or more cities over a period of weeks.

It will be the largest *social* event, too, since tens of thousands of visitors are expected to drop in during June and July of that year, and probably will stay awhile. Because this will be our first appearance on soccer's center stage, we may see *hundreds of thousands* of spectator/visitors.

Actually, we'll be seeing a lot more soccer on television long before 1994, including (thanks to Ted Turner of Turner Broadcasting) the 1990 World Cup from Italy where the U.S. (for the first time since 1950) will appear.

So, my purpose is also to give you an advance perspective of what's in the offing, and resolve a few puzzlements about the soccer you see on television.

You can easily imagine the difficulty I had getting a publisher.

"A book on *soccer* for American and Canadian spectators? Surely you jest, Mr. Cook."

Only an *Englishman*, Anton Rippon of Breedon Books in Derby — pronounced *Darby*, of course — was willing to take the risk, joining forces with Dick Lipsey of SPORTSGUIDE, INC., in Princeton, who publishes *SPORTS MARKET PLACE* and *BASEBALL MARKET PLACE* annually, and Al Zavelle of Cameron Associates, also in Princeton, consultants to publishers.

Together they formed a new venture, Soccer Publishing, Inc., for this and other soccer books to come, including a complete history of the World Cup from 1930 through 1990.

As the leading publisher of soccer books in the U.K. and now expanding into this market, Rippon and his Breedon associates added perspectives I might have missed, and fine-tuned the factual elements. Lipsey and Zavelle, in Princeton, made sure I didn't let my idiosyncratic tendencies get out of hand.

And then there's Ronni Rose who, as Managing Editor with SPORTSGUIDE (and now S.P.I.) and also the mother of youth soccer players, provided yet a different set of perspectives. (Now that she's put aside her red pen I've even begun speaking to her again!)

Creating this book has been a fun and rewarding experience. I hope reading it is equally so.

Where Did "Soccer" Come From?

I SUPPOSE we should take a moment to satisfy historians who insist on knowing when and where things began. But just a moment, because with soccer, nobody knows. The idea of kicking a round object, other than a rock, has to be universal and timeless. Whoever stood upright first upon this earth probably invented some form of the game.

The Chinese had a version (*Tsu Chu*) about 2,500 years ago, and the Japanese copied their Asiatic rivals with what they called *Kemari*. Around the other side of the world, in Classical Greece, there was *Eniokupos*, which the Romans later adopted as *Harpastum*. Any and all such claims to originality can be disputed by paintings vaguely suggestive of the game in ancient Egyptian tombs. Then there are Persian tapestries, Etruscan ruins, and maybe even a yet-to-be-discovered Inca temple of round rather than pyramid shape. Everyone has their own historic origins, and they're welcome to them.

Just to rile up the purists, I used to suggest that credit probably rested with some long-ago-and-hopefully-far-away tribe of headhunters who, with all their display poles occupied, found an innovative and healthful use for their latest trophy. I was kidding, but in 217 A.D. the residents of Derby, England, apparently were not. They used skulls of defunct Roman conquerors for games of kick-around.

Well, at least that's how the story goes. Rippon says it's just folklore — he lives in Derby, after all — and cites the origins of the game we know today as being between two church parishes — St. Peter's and All Saints' — which is where the term "derby" came from, meaning an intense local rivalry. (Fiction or fact . . .I sort of like the former.) At any rate, in 1796, a Derby man called John Snape was killed, "an unfortunate victim to this custom of playing football at Shrovetide."

Even Rippon won't dispute what happened in the tenth century. The residents of Kingston-upon-Thames, near London, celebrating the defeat of a band of Danish marauders, lopped off the Viking captain's head, and had a grisly ball. It's fair to assume, though, that skills and tactics were minimal, and that they had some trouble finding goalkeepers.

Apparently the practice — at that point one could hardly call it a game — caught on and presumably led to this quaintly worded edict by King Edward II a couple of centuries later.

"Foreasmuch as there is a great noise in the city caused by hustling over large balls from which many evils might arise which God forbids, we command and forbid on behalf of the King, on pain of imprisonment, such game to be used in the city in the future."

Contemporary artist's impression of 'mob' football in the streets of Medieval London.

Ed should have realized he was only fanning the flames. Those already hustling after large balls weren't about to stop their pursuit of evils, and those unfamiliar with the practice must have made every effort to check out exactly what evils they had been missing.

Subsequent monarchs including Liz herself had no better luck preventing hustling — what else was there to do for recreation in those times? — so it's hardly a surprise that in the year 1583, Philip Stubber, author of the appropriately titled *ANATOMY OF ABUSES*, noted: "Football is a devilistic pastime with brawling, murder, homicide, and a great effusion of blood . . . ."

Actually, there's a point to be made here. Ancient soccer, much like lacrosse as played by Native Americans, was a lesser form of warfare. Hundreds might chase the bladder (occasionally), and batter each other (constantly) over miles of terrain without rules, and oftentimes without goals.

It wasn't until the ball could be passed that soccer became a game – and that happened only towards the end of the 19th century.

Soccer football, rugby football and football football

EASIER than explaining human behavior, although not a whole lot at that, is clearing up the confusion among names. In Europe, and elsewhere, they still refer to soccer as football, which it is technically, just as what we call football isn't that at all, except that it used to be, and still is upon occasion. (Patience, clarity cometh.)

Things started out all right in England with the roundball game being called football, since the foot was the main propelling instrument. Then, in 1823, a student at the Rugby School named William Webb Ellis, presumably impatient or inept, picked up the ball, and ran with it. History doesn't tell us where he ended up with it, but he started something that took decades to resolve.

Apparently there were advocates of both styles of play so, for the next several years, various groups tried to effect a compromise that would satisfy everyone.

For example, similar to hockey, compromise rules allowed a player to use his hands to bat the ball to the ground and kick it. That's totally illegal today. However, kicking the ball while it was in the air, now intrinsic to the game, was prohibited.

We even see early reference to a term retained in our own football — the "fair catch," which allowed the player to snare it in flight, place it on the ground, and take a running free kick.

Finally, in 1863, the Football Association was founded in London to effect a compromise, but deciding it was impossible, reverted to the original hands-less game. To differentiate, they called it "Association football" which was shortened to "assoc," and eventually soccer.

The new hands-and-anything-else-goes version became rugby (football). Why commemorate the locale rather than the inventor? Perhaps because rugby has an appropriately growling sound while "ellis" doesn't fit however you say it.

Incidentally, it wasn't just handling the ball or not which caused confrontation. There was a school of thought amongst the rugby men that "hacking" — that's kicking people on the shins — should be allowed. The men of Blackheath School (London) held that "hacking is the true football game and if it is done away with, then all the pluck and courage of the game will be at an end." The association men felt that if hacking was allowed then "men of business will be unwilling to play football."

After that 1863 meeting, Blackheath School left the Football Association to form their own group. Strangely, of all the clubs at that earliest meeting, only Blackheath, the rugby club, still exists.

Something few Americans are aware of is that soccer progressed through a similar, and just as popular, evolution in this country late in the 19th century. We assume that American football derived directly from rugby, but that famous first "football" game . . .Princeton versus Rutgers in 1869 . . .was played with a *round* ball that could only be kicked. It was *their* football. Ours was still to come, and when it did, it came from Canada. (Sorry about that.)

In 1874, McGill from Montreal surprised Harvard by running and throwing the ball as well as kicking it. The Crimson thought that was a neat idea, and couldn't wait to pull the same surprise on their Bulldog buddies in New Haven the next year.

In 1886, the anything-but-hands pass was written into the rules — Rippon reminds me they are "laws," but I'll refer to them as rules, since that's the term used for our other sports — by the International Board comprised mainly of British Isles members. (*Trivia - that's why, despite its worldwide purview, soccer dimensions are in yards and feet rather than metric units.*) Not many years later, the anything-but-feet pass became legal in our football. Thus, the sports with common antecedents were forever set off on their different paths.

Their paths also differ in terms of governance. While our team sports have volumes of rules that change constantly, and require almost as many officials as players, soccer has only seventeen rules which, with just one major exception, have remained essentially unchanged.

(Closing Thought)

Soccer still is today what it was a century ago, a totally natural and deceptively simple game for participants. Everything else — *including spectators, coaches, reporters, and even officials in a way* — are incidentals.

Why Are So Many Otherwise Rational People Now Playing Soccer?

IN OUR minds, one of the great mysteries of life is why soccer has always been by far the most popular sport elsewhere in the world to the degree of inspiring near-religious passions.

In *their* minds, and this we prefer to overlook, is curiosity as to why Americans are almost alone in remaining aloof from soccer. After all, 655 *million* people in 166 countries watched Argentina defeat West Germany in the finals of the 1986 World Cup in Mexico City . . .that's one-tenth of the world's population!

Somehow it has become a them versus us situation. Soccer is a "foreign" sport. Yet, we've just noted that soccer initially took hold in this country more than a century ago, and, while pushed by other sports into the background, it never went away.

For example, soccer was played professionally in this country during the first third of this century. Like the North American Soccer League of recent vintage, the early teams were heavily stacked with foreign-born players, but they drew crowds as large as 35,000, which was pretty impressive for those days.

Whether directly the cause, professional soccer couldn't survive the Depression. Perhaps, as newcomers strove to become assimilated into their new homeland they, too, turned to baseball and football. That was the period in our history when we were anxious to establish our own identity in every possible way.

What we see now, as the world draws closer together, is that more than 15 million Americans of all ages, shapes, sizes, and genders (about 40% female, by the way) are soccer players. It's arguably (for once, the word applies) the fastest growing team sport in the country.

To those who maintain that soccer still runs behind softball and volleyball, and will never catch basketball . . ."Hell's bells, as many Americans water ski as play soccer!" . . .I suggest you forget numbers, and concentrate on what is meant by "players."

According to the Soccer Industry Council of America, more than *half* the players participate in at least 25 games per year, the equivalent of both fall and spring league schedules. SICA labels a few million players as "serious," managing to squeeze in more than 50 games a year. (Serious indeed! When do they go on vacation?)

Speaking of vacation, only a couple hundred thousand people can be termed water *skiers.* The other fifteen-plus million, and I'm among them, bounce along on the slats once or twice a year, mostly to be able to brag that they've done it and survived.

To understand why soccer has achieved such grass roots appeal, we have to take a fresh look at the sport and our own society.

We start off in the wrong direction if we think of soccer as being most like field hockey or lacrosse, because those sports have about the same number of people bearing the same positional designations on the same size field doing the same thing, trying to propel a ball into a net. However, there's a major tactical difference —*field hockey and lacrosse players cannot move freely about the field.* Soccer allows, and even insists upon, total freedom of movement.

Nor is soccer more comparable to rugby despite their common antecedents. A rugby ball is similar to a football in shape, control, and shielding, but dribbling skills, which are so much a part of soccer, have litttle significance. A rugby ball can be passed, but only sideways or backwards, never forward.

The more we look and compare, the more evident it becomes that soccer has its own universal popularity counterpart here, which, until recently, may have been equally puzzling to people across the big pond.

Soccer is the rest of the world's BASKETBALL

NOT to belabor the point, but there's another reason the mass influx of immigrants failed to implant soccer over here. Where did almost all of them implant *themselves?* Deep within our major cities, where soccer fields (and grass itself) were at best a rarity, but where pavement abounded.

Despite the obvious *dissimilarities* between the two sports, take a look at what I consider the best in-a-few-words definition of soccer from an unlikely but maybe most appropriate source, the *AMERICAN HERITAGE DICTIONARY*: ". . .in which two teams of 11 men each on a rectangular field with net goals at either end maneuver a round ball mainly by kicking, butting, or using any part of the body except the hands and arms in attempts to score points."

Change just a few words and you've got basketball. Both are totally natural activities based on a very simple premise — using only what you were born with, to maneuver a large round ball, by passing or dribbling, until someone is in position to put it into a net. With hands and no feet in one case, with feet and no hands in the other, but with every other part of the body involved. (I'm sure "butting" means *heading* the ball, but many a goal in soccer is ricocheted off an unsuspecting rear end.)

The only significant difference is *space*. Were conditions reversed, their basketball might have become our soccer.

In Canada, it would be just as appropriate to say that soccer is the rest of the world's *hockey*, by much the same line of reasoning. It doesn't require much space, ice is easy to come by (hard to get rid of!), pucks can be anything you happen to have handy, and even sticks are easy enough to fashion. You really don't even need skates if you have a good sense of balance.

Soccer and basketball are "pick-up" sports

BASKETBALL and soccer are fun and easy to play at the casual level. Neither require any investment beyond a ball and a pair of shoes and sometimes not even those in soccer. (Soccer predates footwear, and, even now, barefoot place-kickers in football are common, because they don't strike the ball with the toe.) Half court and half field pick-up games prevail today as they always have.

Based on one-on-one "keep away" confrontations, short passes, and quick movement to get open, both games can be played with a random number of participants, preferably, but not necessarily, divisible by two. While you do need at least one standard goal for basketball, a couple of jerseys do perfectly well as a soccer (or hockey) goal.

Baseball may be our national pastime, but it's not really a *pick-up* pastime. You really do need some pre-arrangements, since you can't do much without having a regular diamond, and a full complement of players on each side. That these were readily available in small towns, where immigrants seldom settled, and that the game was also invented here, may be the reason our rural grass root is baseball, as our urban "non-grass" root is basketball. (Just a thought in passing . . .don't hold me to it.)

Because open fields were everywhere and almost anything could be kicked around — a bundle of rags, or a blown-up animal bladder first supplanting human skulls — it was inevitable that soccer would have earlier origins in rural societies.

And, because paved areas and gymnasiums, and balls that would bounce with some predictability came later, and in an urban society, so did basketball. In fact, the first basketballs were themselves soccer balls, so soccer can claim some credit for originating what was to become America's most popular team sport.

The reverse trend away from metropolitan cores began after World War II and has been accelerating ever since. Once again, masses of people have access to grassy fields conducive to the rediscovery — for that's what it amounted to — of soccer.

Soccer is in tune with our changing life styles

IN HIS recent book, *VAIN GLORY*, which attempts to explain why football has not been doing well in its Texas heartland, Jan Reid credits (or blames, depending on your outlook) soccer. This passage, quoted in a *Sports Illustrated* review of Reid's work, summarizes why soccer has become "the sport of choice among Texas children of the 1980's" despite the state's football traditions:

"Soccer has caught on in this country in the best and most durable of places — the grass roots. Parks and recreation departments love soccer. It doesn't require expensive facilities and equipment, the risk of injury is slight and kids of any size, gender, and athletic talent can play."

Here again, had Reid been writing several years ago, change "grass roots" (I assume that wasn't intended as a pun) to "play-ground," and he might be describing basketball.

He goes on to attribute the change of athletic choice to the desire by today's youth to break from parental traditions, and, as with rock music, establish their own independent identities. This is one time Dad can't interfere with unwanted advice or criticism. (Sorry, kids, I may be planting some vile thoughts in his mind, but at least he can't bore you to death repeating the story of how he scored the winning goal for Alma Mater.)

Reid was focusing on youth, but what we're seeing is that adults are getting out there on soccer fields, because "*people* of any size, gender and athletic talent can play," as the rest of the world knew all along.

What's happening is characteristic of our times in another way. Instead of parents influencing their kids' choices, kids are influencing their parents' choices. (Mine are the ones who are forcing me to become semi-computer-literate if only to remain a part of their world.)

Also, soccer — yes, like basketball — suits our concerns for health and fitness. Nothing develops the cardiovascular system like the constant and varied aerobics of chasing — and I mean sprinting — around that enormous field. (I have trouble with joggers who join my teams. They don't know *how* to sprint!)

Another change in our life styles is the growing number of two-income families, and the resulting emphasis on "quality time." In decline are sedentary (and sodden) social activities. In ascent are physical activities that blend health benefits with interpersonal relations.

Now there are men's and women's leagues, Over-30 and even Over-40 leagues with national, and in some cases international, titles, being contested. We also see the effect of the feminist movement. Not only are females invading this ultimate male-bastion sport, their numbers are growing faster and our national girls' and women's teams are already among the best in the world.

(Closing Thought)

Here's an old saying that almost predates soccer itself, and supposedly explains sports preferences:

"When you toss a ball at an American toddler he'll try to catch it and throw it back. When you toss a ball at an English toddler he'll try to block it and kick it back."

Even if true . . .and I don't recall any valid hand-eye/foot-eye studies . . .is it really an inherent difference in physical make-up, or a matter of a toddler emulating what he sees Daddy do?

Imagine what might happen when one tries this with a Latin

American or Asian toddler. Since he's likely to be exposed to both soccer *and* baseball, the kid might block the ball, and throw it back, or catch the ball, and kick it back. (If he's a shrewd little devil, he'll ignore the ball, and make Daddy chase it!)

In Soccer, "People Of Any Size Can Excel"

BY altering Jan Reid's commentary from "play" to *excel*, and adding a few years to "kids," we now have, literally this time, another dimension of soccer that helps explain its growing popularity among our young folk.

Where can today's youngster with superior athletic potential concentrate his efforts in hopes of excelling into a professional career? *Unless he's likely to reach excessive physical proportions, his choice is limited, and becoming more so all the time.*

While there are still some football players weighing less than 200 lbs., those not headed for 300 lbs. have slim chances. (Bronko Nagurski was considered a behemoth for his time, but would be considered too small to be a tackle today.) Likewise for basketball, if he's not headed for seven feet. (In time, and, in fact, already, that may be *eight* feet.)

Even hockey and baseball at top levels require beyond-normal size. It may not be too evident on the rink, because stick-handler garb and skates disguise size, but it certainly is evident in baseball, where players are approaching football dimensions. (Can you believe that, at about 180 pounds, Ty Cobb was one of the largest men in the game in his era?)

A similar trend, should our budding young exceller be thinking on all these lines, is occurring in individual sports with professional career potential.

One glance at Becker and Graf tells us that professional tennis is following the trend. (And don't tell me Steffi is only 5 ft. 9 in. I measured myself alongside her one day and can tell you she's close to 6 feet.) With larger and more powerful racquets wielded by larger and more powerful people, the serve is throwing the game out of balance, and occasioning talk about allowing only *one* serve in order to bring things *back* into balance.

So, what's left for the average-sized athlete is soccer.

But, as is so often noted, soccer in this country provides limited, if any, professional career possibilities worth the dedication. This lack has hindered our soccer development, since the talented jocks who might have become our Pelés and Maradonnas have had to switch to something else that would at least pay for college.

Fully mindful of the problem, the United States Soccer Federation is developing a professional league — three of them, actually — that will provide the opportunity. And not for foreign players past their prime — for our own talent. (We'll take a look at this in a later chapter.)

(Closing Thought)

When I started writing this book, I tried to follow non-gender guidelines, because females represent well over one-third of all soccer players in this country, and at this time, are doing better in international competition than their male counterparts. I abandoned use of the third person plural, became its constant use became too clumsy and patently artificial, but I have girls and women very much in mind, because excessive size (and power) are virtually irrelevant in soccer.

Granted, a male team will usually defeat a female team, but it will be on the basis of greater overall speed. Serious co-ed adult leagues in soccer are much in vogue . . .including tournaments . . .but can you imagine co-ed basketball or football beyond a casual level?

Pelé himself once prophesied that at least a few women would eventually be playing in the North American Soccer League. Since the NASL is long-since defunct we'll never know, but I'll top his prophecy — *there will be a professional women's league, and its spectator appeal may surprise a lot of people.*

And, folks, get this – the governing body of international soccer (you'll get to know FIFA shortly) is sponsoring a Women's World Cup for 1991, to take place in *China*, with teams from 16 nations to be invited. Now wouldn't *that* be a fascinating opportunity for an enterprising television bunch!

Why It Seems So Few Goals Are Scored

I ADD "seems" as a qualifier to the above, because soccer gets a bum rap scoringwise. A 3-2 result, common-enough in soccer — hockey, too — is like a 21-14 result in football. And your best-played baseball games are those with the fewest "goals."

Yet it does seem peculiar that so many shots find their way into a basketball net only marginally larger than the ball itself, and so few shots find their way into a soccer net 8 yards wide and 8 feet high. An area of 192 square feet of goal is a lot for any goalkeeper to cover when he represents maybe only 30 square feet with arms and legs outstretched.

Some reasons are apparent. First, a ball can be thrown with greater precision than it can be kicked or headed. Second, a wooden floor or pavement gives a bouncing basketball predictability, while on grass, especially on clumpy fields used by amateurs, a bouncing soccer ball seems to have a self-protective mind of its own. Third, basketballs are lofted out of reach, while a soccer ball, in order to get under that 8 foot high crossbar, usually travels at body level. Most shots ricochet off intervening bodies before they can reach the goalmouth. And, fourth, there's the traffic cop in the goal to bypass. If "goal-tending" were legalized in basketball, every team would have a seven-plus-footer doing little else than creating scoreless games!

What amounts to a fifth reason is that the ball is generally moving *towards* the defense, and therefore, away from attackers. If the ball is in front of them, defenders have time in their favor. At that, they don't have to do much with the ball beyond moving it out of harm's way. If the ball gets behind the field defenders, the goalkeeper enjoys an even greater time advantage to charge out and claim it.

Then there's the offside rule which is as confusing in soccer as it is in ice hockey. We'll examine this in detail, but without knowing

A crowded goalmouth. The forward didn't score. Despite being so close, he was baulked by defenders.

details, you know its purpose — to prevent someone from lurking around the opponent's goal where they can take a long pass and drill it into the net. As you can imagine, without the offside rule, scores would be as high as anyone could possibly want, but the game would be virtually destroyed.

Another reason which we'll also examine in detail is that, like baseball, soccer teams are structured for "strength up the middle." As the intention is to keep runners from reaching second base and scoring position, baseball defense is built upon the catcher, short stop/second base combination, and center fielder, who has the greatest speed, surest glove, and strongest arm.

Since in soccer the idea is to keep shooters away from the goalmouth, the most capable and versatile field players occupy central defensive and midfield roles. When confronted by defenders fast enough to stay with them, and even overtake them, the skill to take the ball away, the size to head away lofted balls, and the experience to mess up their best-laid plans, attackers are often intimidated into shooting before they're ready. Or, as we'll see in a moment, not shooting at all.

Here's yet another reason you may want to evaluate for yourself. *Too many players don't shoot when they do have the chance.* It's not universally true — I've had players who would shoot standing on their heads — but prevalent enough to believe it's a factor, and to be curious as to why.

Believing that, even at upper levels, "a high percentage of opportunities to shoot are missed," Charles Hughes, one-time manager of the English amateur international team, offers what seems to be a likely hypothesis.

"Some consider it one of the mysteries of life why players don't shoot when they are in a position to do so. There is no mystery about it! Teachers and coaches are to blame for encouraging and praising players for their unselfish play. Unselfish players don't win matches.

"Players in shooting positions should accept their responsibility, not only for scoring but also for missing. One cannot have it both ways. The facts are that a player will miss many more times than he will score." (*SOCCER TACTICS AND TEAMWORK,* EP Publishing Limited).

I'm not sure about that unselfish bit. My own guess is that the apparent enormity of the goal is the problem. "How could he have missed?" We understand why the best hitters in baseball fail to connect safely about seven out of ten times, but we tend to forget that, for the reasons we've enumerated, the odds are also against shooters in soccer.

As if there weren't handicaps enough, the very vastness of a soccer field means that the ball takes a while to move from one end of the field to the other. Relatively few shots can be taken and fewer still with any realistic chance of scoring.

Imagine basketball moved from the gym to the great outdoors. Since about *twelve* basketball courts would fit within a soccer field, you'd have *60* players on a side — 120 overall — who still couldn't move the ball fast and far enough to score many baskets. No doubt they'd start kicking it out of frustration, and we'd have the ultimate blend of our two most natural sports. Hands, feet, and anything else — you know, we may have something here!

(Closing Thought)

Those wanting more scoring in soccer may point to a simple and obvious solution — *enlarge the goal.* Making it just one yard wider, or one foot higher, would increase scoring, but by how much, and at what expense?

Those wanting *less* scoring in basketball would "reduce" the goal by raising the hoop one foot. It would change the game considerably with more emphasis on outside shooting, and the virtual elimination of the slam dunk. Is it a better game? It's a matter of personal opinion.

In soccer, it comes down to why the soccer goal was created in its 8 yards by 8 foot dimensions. That's worth a closer look a little later.

Scoring Isn't What You Come To Watch Anyway

TO knowledgeable spectators, the scoring of a goal is sometimes irrelevant — an anti-climax. They come to watch the chess-like sequences of events, and the individual initiatives that usually result in an ultimate confrontation in or near the goalmouth. A last-instant clearance by a fullback, or a diving deflection by a goalkeeper, may itself be a climax, like an open field tackle or tipped pass that prevents a touchdown.

Of 125 plays in football, each its own sequence of events, at most ten result in goals, and they may be anti-climactic to what occurred before. Just as most soccer action occurs outside the penalty areas, most football action occurs outside the 20-yard lines.

If there are 70 "plays" in baseball, how many result in runs? Most meaningful action relates to baseball's penalty area — second base — the offense trying to get players into scoring position, and the defense trying to hold them short.

In coming chapters, we'll cover tactics, but since they depend on ball control, let's first see what "using any part of the body except hands and arms" means in terms of individual skills and athleticism.

The foot can make the ball do all kinds of tricks

WE think of soccer being a matter of kicking a ball — "us guys this way, you guys that way." Even if that's all there were to it, there are many different ways to kick, and not to kick, like with the toe. Toe kicks have limited power and accuracy, and besides, they destroy the toenails.

The basic kick is with the instep. With the leg forming a straight line from knee down, the foot becomes a mallet, and the ball is driven forward off the laces. Try this ballet-like pose yourself, and

Kicking or passing with the inside and outside of the foot "off the laces."

you'll discover it requires extreme flexibility. ("Sasquatch" — Big Foot — might be a great football or basketball player, but he'd be a lousy soccer player, except maybe in the goal.)

Leaning over the ball, and striking it amidship, produces a line drive. Leaning back a bit, and striking it lower, lofts the ball. Striking it in the upper half causes the ball to scoot along the ground. That's simple physics, although no cinch when the ball's in motion.

There are times when one wants to curve or "bend" the ball, like a baseball pitcher, perhaps to sneak it past the keeper or swing it along the sideline. Simple physics again — striking the ball at an angle to give the ball right or left spin during flight.

It's possible to swerve the ball either way, depending on whether you hit it with the inside or outside of your foot. The Brazilians perfected the art and became famous for the "banana" shot.

Then there's the volley kick of a bouncing ball which is an essential skill, because especially in front of the goal, most balls are in fact above the ground. Like its tennis namesake, the volley is a quick punch.

It's the hardest kick to master, because of the added dimension of height. When the ball is alongside, it's a matter of rotating the hips, and swinging the foot in a horizontal arc to power the ball off the laces — and often ending up sprawled on the turf. When the ball is in front of him, the player may have to leap to drive the ball horizontally, rather than over the bar.

Hard as it is to do all these things with one foot, the accomplished player has to be equally adept, or nearly so, with *both* feet. Soccer balls are seldom considerate enough to nestle on your favorite side.

Whereas kicks are normally off the laces, passes come off the sides of the foot — the inside or outside depending on which way the player wants to direct the ball. Even the heel, or the bottom of the foot, come into play when one wants to push the ball backwards.

Since the ball spends a lot of time off the ground, volleying techniques are vital.

Trapping is catching without hands

TO get the ball on the foot may first require "trapping" the ball with whatever part of the body is appropriate, and "settling" the ball within easy reach on the ground. There's a direct corollary to "soft hands" by a wide receiver.

To teach a neophyte to trap, I sometimes fake a punch at their gut, which causes an instinctive collapsing response. "Perfect — that's just what to do when the ball comes into your mid-section. By softening the impact you allow the ball to drop at your feet." Conversely, stiffening the stomach muscles causes the ball to deflect out of reach. (I don't know if mine is accepted coaching technique, but it works.)

When the ball comes sailing towards the chest, instead of collapsing forward, the player has to collapse *backwards* as though doing the limbo. Less instinctive, and harder to learn, but with the same reasoning — in effect, to catch the ball with the body, rather than deflect it away.

Trapping and settling a grounder follows the same softening-of-impact principles, only they may be even harder to apply. The knee becomes a kind of hinge allowing the foot to swing back with the ball, and calm it down. When the ball is alongside, there's always the danger of it hopping over the foot so, rather than just stick the foot out at an angle, the leg should be kept perpendicular. Now, when in motion, that's really hard to do.

Just as receivers in football must have "soft hands," soccer players must have a soft *touch* with everything (except their hands) to keep the ball within easy reach. Thus, trapping with chest, instep, knee and sole are all ways of cushioning the ball.

Heading goes against all sense of self-preservation

WHEN a ball or anything else comes flying at our heads, we close our eyes and duck. A soccer player has to keep his eyes wide open, and stick his head — and maybe his face — in front of a ball that might be travelling, and tumbling like something from Roger Clemmons. (Even if helmets and face masks were allowed, all control would be lost.)

Even heading isn't as obvious as it may seem. True, most of the time the idea is to bang it straight off the forehead, but the head can also be used to direct the ball sideways, or even flip it

No, this guy did not handle the ball, but the photograph shows the rough and tumble of aerial combat on the soccer field.

Even professionals close their eyes occasionally. These World Cup stars don't seem to know where the ball is.

further along the way it's going, and keep it out of reach of the opposition.

When players leap for a head, they have to coordinate, and time everything perfectly. Too soon, and they get it in the face. Too late, and the ball grabs a hunk of hair. Either way, it smarts.

Space gives an extra dimension to dribbling

THAT it's also termed "carrying the ball" suggests that there's more to soccer dribbling than basketball dribbling. The idea is the same, to deceive an opponent into committing the wrong way, or at the wrong time, but with the added dimension of *space* — in all directions, including UP. A player can pass to *himself*, pushing the ball past a challenger, or even flipping it over his head, and taking off after it. (Nothing riles this challenger more than a pass between his legs. That's why there's no three-point stance in soccer.)

One Britisher was so good at dribbling in the open field that they named the "Stanley Matthews" maneuver in his honor. He would fake one way, step over the ball with one foot, and poke it the other way with the inside of the trailing foot. (It defies illustration, but you might have someone show it to you.)

(Closing Thought)

To fully appreciate individual skills, add in the presence of opposing players, also trying to kick, pass, trap, head, and dribble the same ball at the same time. *"Move To The Ball!"* — that's the rallying cry of soccer mentors the world over. The player who waits for the ball to come to him may not get it. He has to move quickly towards the ball, which adds to the pace he has to deal with when trying to do something with it. The same is true with our soft-hands wide receiver, but a football follows a predictable path. A soccer ball refuses to.

A Cook's Tour Of A Soccer Field

SINCE my objective is to paint the picture of soccer in bold strokes, and leave the subtle shadings for others more qualified than I, in the next few chapters we'll brush off (sorry, that one's an accident) most of the how-to rules of the game to give clear form to the two essential rules that you should understand.

Just for the record, and because we'll be encountering "Feefah" (FIFA) periodically, since 1904 the game has been under the control of the *Federation Internationale de Football Association* headquartered in Switzerland. And, if you want to call soccer rules *laws*, that's okay with me, since that *is* the proper term. As I said earlier, where there are differences in terminology between them and us, I'll favor whichever helps the understanding process.

As it happens, Rule 1 which lays out the playing area also has just two significant elements — *overall dimensions and the penalty areas.* All the other elements are trivial, and/or self-evident.

One aspect of soccer that takes us some getting used to is that fields can vary considerably in size and shape. It may be anywhere from 100 to 130 yards long, and from 50 to 100 yards wide. Probably FIFA wanted to accommodate the areas that might be available in crowded European and British communities, but such variance does influence play.

You may also be aware that the field is still called the "pitch" in the U.K. and elsewhere. I've often wondered if they didn't mean the term literally, as when a ship plunges through turbulent seas. Being so large, soccer fields are seldom level (but *always* windy). Most do indeed resemble a freeze-action shot of the deck of an old four-master in rough weather.

Theoretically the field could be 100 yards *square*. It can't, because the laws/rules further define the field as "rectangular" such that the length must be greater than the width. Perhaps someone a century ago foresaw teams getting confused, and playing from side to side rather than end to end.

The field can also be more than twice as long as it is wide, 130 by 50 yards. I don't recall seeing one with this elongation, but you can understand how the two extremes would result in two entirely different games.

Perhaps anticipating something like this, FIFA states that international matches must be played on fields between 70 and 80 yards in width. This seems a reasonable compromise, but poses a problem in this country where oftentimes, especially in high schools and colleges, soccer gets crammed into football fields.

A football field is much too narrow

THERE'S no problem with length, but at 53$^{1}/_{3}$ yards (160 feet) in width — just barely acceptable for soccer — it is roughly 16 to 26 yards too narrow for the international game.

So what's the big deal about a few yards? An entire style of play, that's what, which hampers our players during their most important developmental years. Youth brought up on proper fields in community programs actually have to *unlearn* how to play soccer when they enter high school.

With limited lateral space, they charge up and down the middle of the field playing "kick and run" without a clue about playing the sidelines, redirecting attacks across the field, and spreading the game out.

On the closer confines of a small field, players receiving the ball have to get rid of it quickly, with little time to set something up. It's hack or be hacked, which is a destructive, rather than constructive style of play.

Suppose, just to draw one of many possible parallels, we were to bring up our tennis aspirants on a singles court 20 feet wide instead of the prescribed 27 feet. How would they do in international competition? "Serve and volley," the racquet equivalent of "kick and run," is all they'd know. They'd be sitting ducks for angled cross-court and down-the-line passing shots.

Bluntly put, if we expect to become competitive in soccer – and if spectators are going to see the game the way it can and should be played – we have to get soccer off football fields. (Maybe, with the sizes and speeds of today's player, it's time to play football on soccer fields.)

The outcome is decided within the penalty areas

THE center line, and that 10 yard circle around its midpoint, look impressive, but they only define where teams line up for "restarts" at the beginning of each period, and after goals.

The center line also relates to the offside rule which we'll examine later. (A player cannot be offside in his own half of the field, which is what you'd expect anyway. Too bad the other aspects of that rule aren't as simple!)

The penalty areas, sometimes called "boxes," measure 18 by 44 yards, and who knows how they came up with those oddball dimensions. A measurement of 20 by 45 yards would be a lot easier to remember, and wouldn't have altered the game one whit, but I suppose there must have been a reason. Whatever, they are critical markings.

Without going into details yet, just be aware that the penalty area serves two basic purposes. It defines where the goalkeeper can use his hands: inside, yes, outside, no. And, it defines where a major foul by the defense results in a penalty-kick from the 12-yard spot indicated on the diagram. (Those little arcs off the outer penalty-lines keep other players 10 yards away from the point where the penalty-kick is taken.)

No other sport has anything like the penalty-kick. A point-blank shot from 12 yards out, it's like stopping a boxing match, and awarding one contestant a free swing at the other's jaw. About 85% of all penalty-kicks score, a substantial number amounting to knock-outs in a relatively low-scoring game.

The penalty area is akin to the 20-yard line in football. It's where the offense wants to get to yet, once there, it's the hardest area to score from for much the same reason — *too many bodies in too little space.* In both games, it's hard to break through a stacked defense.

Located within the penalty area is the goal area (also a "box") — 6 by 20 yards — which serves no other purpose than locating the ball for goal-kicks by the defense. Seems to me a couple of

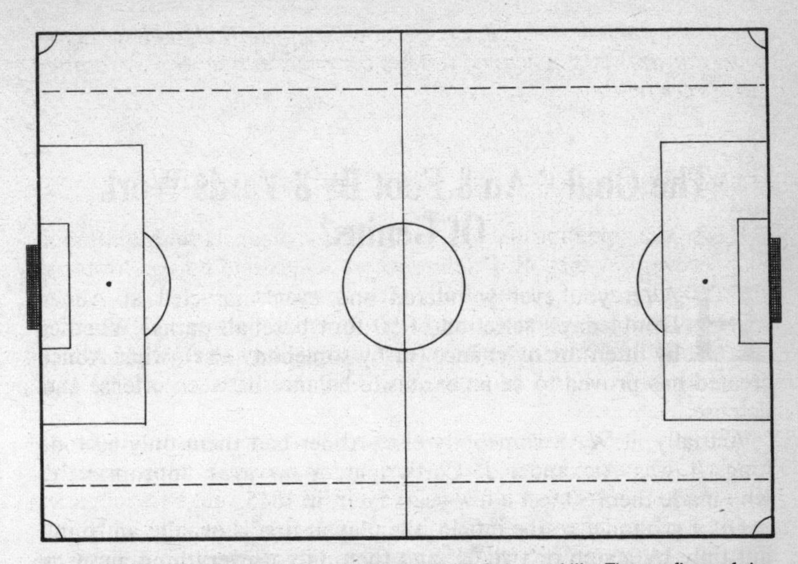

Soccer played on football fields is a bad way to develop our skills. The confines of the football field (indicated by the broken lines) are much narrower than the soccer pitch. Players tend to play "kick and run" up and down the middle rather than spreading the game to the sidelines and building up attacks where there is more space.

blobs of white stuff at the corners would do nicely, but FIFA never consulted me.

Finally, there are those quarter-circle arcs of one-yard radius in each of the four corners. You can figure their purpose, where balls are placed down for corner-kicks. Oh, yeah, the corner-flags . . .they topple if you breathe on them, but while upright, help the referee determine whether a ball goes out over the sideline (touch-line to use proper lingo) or the endline.

(Closing Thought)

Artificial turf didn't exist when soccer rules were laid down, but it is infiltrating soccer as it has baseball and football. Nevertheless, FIFA insists on natural grass for international play.

Those U.S. cities with artificial surfaces in their stadiums will have to provide suitable width and grass if they want to host some 1994 World Cup games.

The Goal – An 8 Foot By 8 Yards Work Of Genius?

HAVE you ever wondered and even marveled at Abner Doubleday's selection of 90 foot baseball paths? Whether by intent or by chance (or by somebody else), what Abner created has proved to be an exquisite balance between offense and defense.

Actually, it WAS somebody else. Abner had them only 60 foot long. It was Alexander J. Cartwright, a *surveyor* appropriately, who made them 90 feet a few years later, in 1845.

Off a grounder to the infield, the play at first is usually an "out," but only by a step or two . . .and then only if everything happens in routine fashion. Anything out of routine — a difficult or muffed pickup, bad throw, speedy batter — can swing the balance towards the offense. So, too, can an outstanding defensive play and/or a lead-footed batter shift the balance further in favor of the defense.

There's an equally exquisite balance between the base runner trying to steal second, and the catcher trying to throw him out — a split-second affair — and between the guy on third tagging up, and sprinting for home on a routine fly to the outfield.

What would baseball be if Cartwright hadn't happened along when he did, or if he himself had opted for 80 feet or 100 feet? Games lasting forever with a deluge of runs, or brief encounters with everyone swinging for the bleachers — baseball wouldn't have survived either way.

We can also wonder at the size and height of the basketball hoop that placed such emphasis on precision shooting, and argue the merits of raising it to restore what seems to have been lost through player elongation.

The dimensions of a soccer goal create a similar kind of balance predicated on the fact that a human being can cover more lateral space by diving than vertical space by jumping.

When everything happens in routine fashion, the shooter is usually

Goalkeeper and fellow fullbacks defend the goal.

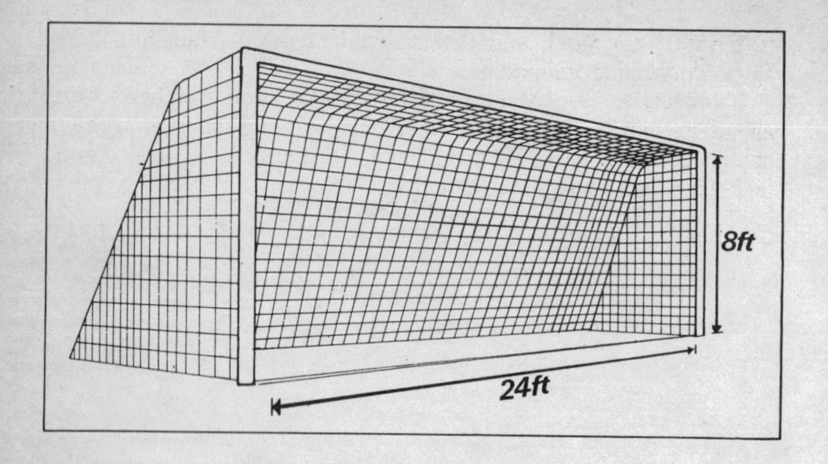

"out" by a narrow margin. But, an ill-timed or misdirected move by the keeper, or a superior shot by an opponent, can upset the balance and result in a goal. Because the odds favor the keeper, most goals are scored off a quick pass resulting in a shot with the keeper out of position.

Suppose the Alexander Cartwright of soccer, whoever he may have been, and nobody seems to know, had set the crossbar at 9 feet and the uprights only 7 yards apart?

Almost the same area of goalmouth, but the result would favor defense even more. Few keepers would be able to block hard shots just below the crossbar, yet they'd be able to nab most shots directed just inside the uprights. Chances are there would be even *fewer* goals, since getting the right elevation on the kick is harder than getting the right angle. Few shots along the ground would reach the net.

Chances are, we'd see more shots being taken, but they'd be long boomers of greater hazard to the spectators than the goal. What we'd lose would be maneuvering that sets up the quick close-in thrust. Power would predominate over quickness.

Change the shape to 7 feet by 9 yards, and the balance is skewed towards the attacker. Ignoring low-percentage air-balls, he'd concentrate on grounders knowing that even a poorly-struck ball close to the post would have a good chance. What we'd likely see would remind us of lacrosse — a bunch of people milling around in front of the goal, and the midfield merely a transition zone. Luck would predominate over all.

However, because there is pressure to make soccer a higher-scoring affair, we may eventually see a larger goal being the *second* major change in FIFA rules, the first being the change in the offside rule in 1925, which we'll get to later.

Who's Who And Why's Why

FIFA Rule #2 makes it clear that it's good to have a ball to play with, but I think we can assume that, and proceed to Rule #3. This one seems equally simple, that there should be 11 players per side, but it's worth clarifying terminology before going further.

I want to say more about the goalkeeper in a moment, but point out now that, instead of our short form "goalie," in soccer it becomes "keeper," and for a reason.

Rather than just deflect shots, hockeylike, his job is to try to gain possession of the ball, and become the first element in the attack. With no playing space behind the goal, a deflect either goes over the endline, which gives the other team a corner-kick, a dangerous opportunity as we'll see in a later chapter, or puts the ball back into play right in front of the goalmouth — more dangerous still. ("Garbage goals" may not impress, but they count just like an ooohhh boomer.)

Once in possession, he "keeps" the ball until his own field players (that's everyone else on his team) has had time to move out where they can take and receive a kick or throw, or at least prevent the other team from launching another attack.

The ten field players break down into defense, midfield, and offense. Let's run through some commonly-used definitions that we'll use as we proceed. To simplify matters, we'll assume four defenders, three midfielders, and three "offenders."

In defining positions we run head-on into differences in terminology. Usually it's a matter of "them," being in the forefront of soccer evolution, altering player designations to adhere to new tactics, while "us," still trying to catch up to the pack, are slower to change.

Defense – only for the "few good men"

Sweeper: As the term implies, he's the player closest to the goal, and most directly responsible for preventing shots by "sweeping" the ball away. Rather than "mark" — cover or guard — any one attacker, he has to pick up whoever breaks past the rest of the defense, which means he's often matched against the most dangerous scorer. If you're partial to Italian, you can call him a "libero," which suggests freedom to sweep where needed.

Right and Left Fullbacks: Traditionally shortened to "backs," they occupy defensive positions on their respective sides of the field,

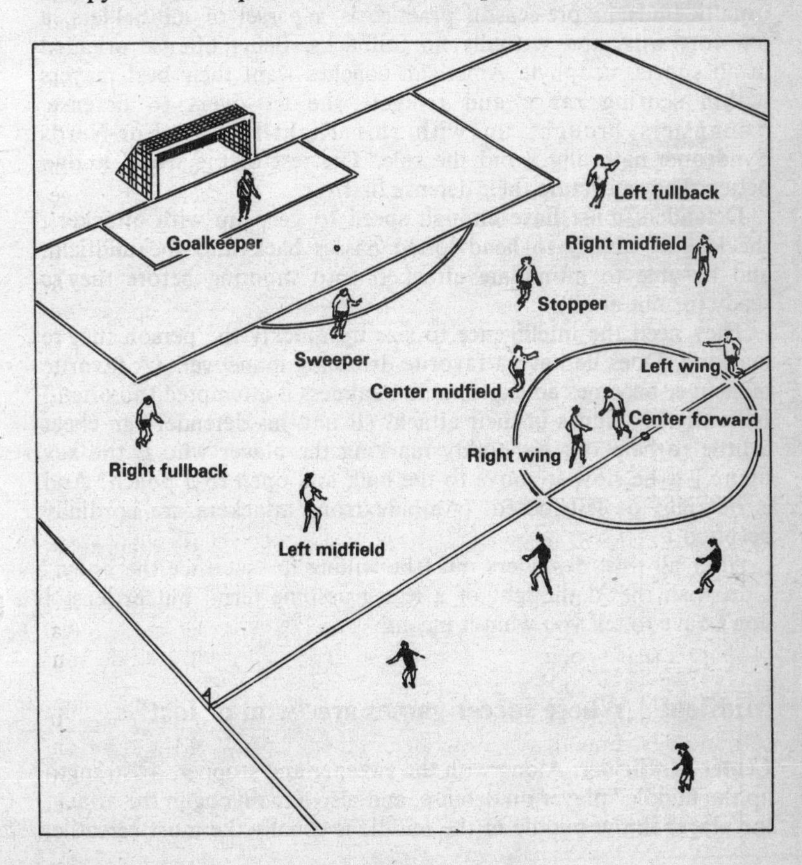

and mark the opposing outside attackers — usually wings, but sometimes attacking midfielders. As such, they may be called "wing" or "outside" backs.

Stopper: This is an ambivalent position, since the stopper may also be called the advance or forward stopper, which suggests a semi-offensive role. Located ahead of the sweeper, this laddie or lassie is primarily responsible for breaking up attacks before they reach threatening proportions, and setting a counter-attack in motion. (In a three-defender pattern, the stopper becomes the *Center Fullback*, and functions as a blend of stopper and sweeper.)

"How come none of you jokers is a fullback?" What a coach usually finds in pre-season practice is a passel of midfielders, a few forwards, and virtually no fullbacks. Being offense oriented in all sports, neophyte American coaches want their best players within scoring range and relegate the left-overs to defense. Youngsters brought up with this Right-Field-Is-For-Nerds Syndrome naturally avoid the role. The rest of the world knows better. They structure their defense first.

Defenders must have enough speed to keep up with attackers, the leaping ability to head lofted passes back into the midfield, and be able to intimidate attackers into shooting before they're ready (or not at all).

They need the intelligence to size up quickly the person they're marking. Does he have a favorite dribbling maneuver? (A favorite maneuver becomes an exploitable weakness if attempted too often.) Is he the key figure in their attack? (If not, his defender can cheat a little to help out his buddy marking the player who *is* the key figure.) Is he slow to move to the ball, and open to a poach? And is he right or left-footed. (Ambidextrous attackers are cordially despised.)

After all this, defenders must be willing to "sacrifice the body." I do wish they'd thought of a less gruesome term, but at least I don't have to tell you what it means.

Midfield – Where soccer games are "won or lost"

Center Midfielder: Along with the sweeper and stopper, a "strength up the middle" player on defense, and also a main cog in the attack, the player in the middle of the middle is usually the most versatile, and most active player on the team. In addition to being where more action occurs than anywhere else, he must be ready to drop back to support the defense, and seconds later, be setting up (if not actually participating), in scoring thrusts sixty-or-more yards away.

Right and Midfielder: Located in outside positions corresponding to right and left fullbacks, these players also provide "links" (that's another, and very apt, term for midfielders) between defense and offense on their sides, including sprinting along the sidelines into wing positions when that player is otherwise occupied.

In case you're wondering, in our lingo, midfielders may still be known as "halfbacks." This time I'll go along with the rest of the world, maybe just to prove that I can.

In addition to sheer skill, know-how, and endurance, I look for a special attribute in midfielders — *a sense of dynamic spatial relations.*

Because linksmanship is so physically demanding, players can only be effective by possessing an instinctive sense of where and when things are *going* to happen. I say "possessing" since, in my experience, while the instinct may be acquired, there's no substitute for being born with it.

For example, knowing where a kick by either keeper will come down, and being there when it does. Figuring where an opponent under attack is likely to pass the ball, and edging into position to intercept it without forewarning an opponent by moving too soon. Anticipating the need to cover for a teammate caught out of position or bypassed by an opponent. Timing a pass beyond the defense just when a forward is poised to make his break.

Like chess, soccer in the midfield is composed of a series of moves that may seem peripheral to any purpose. Players able to think three or four moves ahead can compensate for other deficiencies.

Better to amble to where the ball will be than to sprint to where it was - sort of a truism for life, isn't it?

Offense – only for a few good crazies

Center Forward: Positioned in the middle of the offense, and therefore, likely to score the most goals, these are the fellows — like Pelé and Maradonna — we hear the most about. Since defenses

The game's greatest player? Pelé of Brazil.

key on the center forward — he's the immediate responsibility of the stopper — he has to be agile and quick. Most goals come off momentary openings, the ball on his foot for the briefest moment, so he also must possess a sense of balance to get off shots whenever, and however the opportunity arises. Where four forwards are employed, instead of a center forward, there will usually be a *left and a right Inside.*

Right and Left Wing: Their primary job is to enable other strikers to strike by directing the ball from the sideline or corner across the goalmouth. Whether pursuing a long pass or breaking open themselves with the ball, speed is their essential asset. Seeing an opportunity — laxness by their defender, a midfielder breaking through, and drawing their defender away, an attack being developed from the other sideline — they may swerve towards the goal, and in effect, become "inners."

By the way, when I employ a fourth forward — usually when trying to make up a one-goal deficit late in the game — it's as what I call a *Trailing Forward.* I doubt you'll encounter it elsewhere but I like having a power shooter a few yards behind my center forward to corral balls poorly cleared by the defense, and slightly apart from the madding throng, able to drive a shot over their heads. Besides, two inners tend to get in each other's way or play Alphonse-and-Gaston with a loose ball. (I figure I should leave my own mark on the game before I depart.)

Forwards have to be a little bit nasty, and quite a bit crazy. Because the penalty is trivial, a foul committed by the offense close to the opponent's goal is often a risk worth taking. Shoving a defender to get at the ball, kicking the ball out of the keeper's hands, or even surreptitious use of hands as occurred in the Finals of the 1986 World Cup, if undetected, can lead to a goal that otherwise wouldn't happen. And, if detected, so what? All that happens is a free-kick for the defense from that spot which is probably 80 yards from the other goal.

Since forwards are vulnerable in the act of shooting, it's possible the official will call the foul on the defense, and then a goal is almost forewritten. (Leo Durocher might have been a soccer forward in a previous life.)

Goalkeepers Are The Only Specialists In Soccer

CONSIDERING the similarities of the balls, one might think basketball players would make ideal keepers, because of their height, their leaping ability, and their ball-handling skills. Maybe volleyball players even more so because they combine these attributes with the ability to leap or dive, and spike the ball at the same time. (Literally leap and spike an aerial ball before an attacker can head it in.)

Actually, it's neither of the above, unless they also play soccer. There are occasions when the keeper has to venture beyond the penalty area, and function as a fielder player (and run like hell back to safety!) And once in control of the ball he has to do something with it, like punt it, which isn't so easy if you're not foot-oriented.

I once saw a keeper take a vicious boot, drive the ball about 40 yards straight up, and, luckily for her — yeah, it was one of my girls' teams — catch it again without moving. It must have been a "first" for everyone, including the keeper. Players on both teams just stood gaping, and the referee couldn't think of any rule prohibiting it. (He might have called stalling if he'd stopped laughing long enough.)

It worked out fine that one time — with remarkable aplomb she heaved it out to a teammate as though it had been planned all along — but a keeper's inability to "clear" the ball makes coaches very nervous.

Almost as important as physical capabilities is the keeper's grasp of the entire game. He has to know how to play his own position, and being the only player always facing the action, also act as Secretary of Defense.

The hardest thing for any neophyte keeper to learn is *when* to come out of the goal to intercept a crossing pass, grab off a ball that gets through or over his defense, and especially when to come out to cut off a shooter's angle. Too soon or too late almost *gives* a goal away.

Punching the ball one or two-handed, tipping it over the crossbar or catching it — all important parts of a keeper's repertoire.

Since he's the only player more or less stationary, and facing the action, the keeper must anticipate how a threat will develop, and warn defenders. It is the same if he detects an attacker sneaking into open space and unmarked. (On top of everything else, he needs a good set of lungs!)

And, when he has the ball, he should know how best to initiate a counter-thrust. That long punt or drop-kick looks impressive, but sometimes he can accomplish more by rolling the ball to a wing fullback, or throwing it — hurling it is what they do — to a midfielder in open space by a sideline.

". . .And please be kind to your goal keepers."

I CAN'T leave the subject without quoting Bob Hauser, a professional coach from Czechoslovakia by way of Germany, who taught me much of what I know, and who, after reading this book, will probably deny he ever met me.

The goalkeeper has to be brave as attackers and defenders alike can knock him about when the heat is on.

Conducting a seminar for new coaches of community teams, he amplified his opening remark about the care and feeding of goalkeepers.

"You will find that they feel badly enough if they allow a goal even though it may not have been their fault at all."

Of course, goalkeepers in any sport are vulnerable to mistakes by others, but they are more vulnerable in soccer, at least to suffering blame, since the scoring process is slow-developing, and often obscure.

We seldom point a finger at a forward who failed to recover a ball lost to a defender 80 yards away which results in a score 30 seconds later. And, we forget there's not much even the most acrobatic keeper can do about a well-executed shot from close range.

We also forget that bouncy balls on a bumpy terrain do strange things — and weather conditions make them do stranger things. When wet, not only is the ball slick, it may also scoot lower than expected through the keeper's legs. On a dry, hard terrain, a lazily-lofted ball can jack-rabbit over the keeper's upraised hands.

Chances are, the keeper will be about like everyone else on his team — although one of the taller specimens. You can tell who he is, though, by the outlandish jersey, the mud and/or grass stains, the assorted scars from colliding with posts, elbows, and cleats, and the imprint of the ball etched on chest and cheekbone.

Dave Butz when with the Washington Redskins, in his characteristically to-the-point style, once said, "Football hurts." With no more protection than gloves and knee-pads, so does goalkeeping.

We Disagree With FIFA Over Substitutions

VIEWING amateur games in this country, you may not realize that by allowing unlimited substitutions we are at odds with FIFA. They allow only *two* substitutions during international matches, and at most five under any circumstances, and with an added stipulation — *that once a player is removed from the game he cannot return.*

Presumably, the FIFA rationale is that conditioning and endurance should be an integral, if not dominant, part of the game. Furthermore, and still hypothesizing, the game is so dependent on players working in close harmony that moving people in and out reduces team efficiency. Probably many, if not most, coaches at international and professional levels wouldn't use more subs even if they could . . .(the Quarterback Mind-Set of American football coaches!)

It's bad enough that it's unfair to non-starters who put in the same number of practice hours as anyone else to no purpose. (If I take someone on a team, they get to play every game, at least for a while. I've violated my own edict just *twice*, and the other players chewed me out.) The non-returnable rule is at least as unfair, and potentially harmful, to starters. They have to stay out there even if injured, but still mobile, or badly in need of a rest. And how does this stay-out-there-and-suffer policy jibe with maintaining level of play?

I want to call your attention to the fact that, even with unlimited substituting, coaches may still have a hard time moving people in and out properly. Other than for an injury when only that one player can be replaced, or after a goal, the only time a coach can substitute is when the ball goes out of bounds, and his team has possession — goal-kick, throw-in, or corner-kick . . .(details yet to come). Some 10 or 15 minutes can go by with no such opportunity!

I'm not the only one who feels that substitution rules should be loosened up. Some leagues, here and elsewhere, are experimenting with compromises, such as allowing a specified number of substitutes *without* team possession, and with players allowed to return later.

Substitution — number-3 comes off and is replaced by number-18.

The *Real* Rules Of Soccer

AS many a knowledgeable "soccerist" person will tell you, while there may be 17 rules in all, there are really only *two* that matter — *the offside rule which affects team tactics, and the fouls' rule which governs individual play.* All others, like the first three we've looked at already, cover routine stuff. However, since you may be spectating at a level from beginners to pros, I'll run through all of them in terms of how they may be applied under different circumstances. Hang on, here we go.

Rule #4, defining player equipment, deals only with footwear that might injure someone. If you ever get a chance, read this one if only for its sociological implications. The FIFAites go on and on about "studs," spelling out in minute detail acceptable materials, location, and number, length, maximum and minimum diameter, taper, shape, etc. One must assume soccer in those days had its share of Ty Cobbs, who, with a file, would turn footwear into lethal weapons.

What the rule-makers couldn't foresee were females on the field, or today's masculine adornment, so referees now pay less heed to footwear than to bodywear that could harm the wearer or an opponent. "Please remove all rings, watches, pins, earrings, bracelets, brass knuckles . . ."

The fifth and sixth rules define the role of the officials, and I consider them sufficiently important to be dealt with in a separate chapter.

The next few rules are also pretty cut-and-dry. Games are two 45-minute halves except when reduced for younger teams. Start of play is an indirect free-kick from the center of the field, which means two players have to touch it before it can be advanced. The ball is out of play when it is *totally* over the sideline or endline. And a goal is scored when the ball is *totally* over the goal line between the uprights.

Now we get to the guts of the matter – offsides (#11) and personal fouls (#12).

#12 – OFFSIDE is the only rule ever changed substantively

WHAT'S fascinating here is that only *one* word was changed, yet it altered the game drastically, certainly for the better. Before passing was allowed there was no offside rule at all, because it wasn't needed. The offside rule as originally written amounted to defensive overkill, I would think, because there had been no precedent to draw from.

A player is offside if he is nearer his opponent's goalline than the ball at the moment the ball is played unless:

(a) He is in his own half of the field of play.

(b) There are *three* opponents nearer their own goal line than he is.

(c) The ball was last played by an opponent or was played by him.

(d) He receives the ball direct from a goal-kick, a corner-kick, a throw-in, or when it is dropped by the referee.

That's it, all they wrote. They devoted three times as many words to studs! Rule #11 is a skillful work of precision wording which is easy to understand. Applying it in a constant-action game, where ball and bodies follow no predictable patterns, is something else.

Taking the simple part first: (d) means that there are four situations where the offside rule is waived. Goal-kicks, corner-kicks, and throw-ins are defined by separate rules, which we'll get to in proper sequence, but you may wonder why and when a referee would drop the ball. (The International Board was talking literally. In those days the figurative meaning hadn't been invented.)

It doesn't happen often, but occasionally he may be unable to pinpoint who last touched the ball before it went out of bounds. Or maybe he's had to stop play for some reason like a dog getting into the action.

Then, like a hockey face-off, to restart the game he drops the sphere between two opposing players, and lets them flail away after it touches the ground.

In (b) I highlighted three (the number of opponents nearer the goal line), because that's the substantive word. One of the three would be the keeper, but that still meant an attacker usually faced a two-on-one confrontation to remain on-side. In 1925, scoring was becoming more difficult, as some tactically-aware defenders in the English League devised what amounted to an almost foolproof offside "trap." So, the International Board reduced three to *two*, and that set up the one-on-one confrontations which are such a vital ingredient in the modern game. (Note the parallel in professional basketball — no zone defenses allowed so that one-on-one challenges can predominate.)

Offensive players are safe if they make sure that the ball, or one opposing fullback, is visibly (from the referee's vantage-point) ahead of them, but that's not how most goals are scored. More often they're set up by a quick through-pass (meaning through the defense), or lofted pass over the defense, that a fast forward can overtake and shoot.

But to make that work, the forward has to be barely onside, which translates into *almost offside* at the instant the ball is kicked. And, that's where the troubles start.

In the scenario above, the forward in the dark shirt is offside, perhaps anticipating a through pass too soon. Had he waited a split-second longer he could have run on to the ball from an onside position.

It's such a close call that even professional linesmen can err. When uncertain they tend to favor the defense, which is both annoying and frustrating for offensive players. And, where there are only volunteer linespeople, the referee usually reserves the right to make the call himself from wherever he happens to be at the time. Since that may be a ways away, he's likely to "see it" in favor of the defense.

Wait a darn minute, Cook. The rule states that an attacker only needs to be onside "at the moment the ball is played." Once a teammate boots the ball goalward, he's permitted to get ahead of the ball itself, or the last defender. That's what the fast break, or through-pass, is all about, isn't it?

True, but that's seldom the way the rule is applied in a game with just one official, and you can't count on three officials getting it right. So, while a player gives up a yard or so, he still has the advantage, since he's heading the right way, while the defender has to turn and run, or back-pedal.

Look, except on free-kicks, the referee's likely to be — he should be! — in the area of the ball when it's struck. He's in no position to determine if a player 30 yards away, and at a bad angle, was (in fact), onside at that precise moment. What he *can* see, out of the corner of his eye from a distance, is someone dashing madly goalward all alone. Not sure, he's likely to play it safe and blow the play dead.

The thought may occur to you that a soccer referee should judge the offside like a first base umpire. Unable to watch ball and bag simultaneously, he points his nose towards the bag, and listens for the ball hitting the glove. So, all the referee has to do is watch the offensive player, and listen for the sound. At least that's the theory.

One difference is that while the umpire is a few feet from a loud *"thwock,"* the referee may be several yards away from a quiet thud. Another, is that he may have to watch two or three people poised to break at once. Linesmen have the opposite problem. They can track player positions, but are too far away to be sure precisely when the ball is kicked.

Given all this hoopla, you might notice teams conducting tests in the early minutes. They deliberately violate the offside rule slightly, and see what happens. If they get away with it, they have a tactical edge, and may score an early goal. If they get whistled, they may next test the referee by being just barely onside at the time of the kick.

If they still get whistled, however wrongly, at least they know how the referee operates. Then they can adapt, rather than have attacking thrusts constantly whistled to a stop.

Isn't this a form of cheating? No more so than a pitcher testing a home plate umpire by nibbling around the plate in the first couple of innings to find out what he will call. Every umpire has a slightly different strike zone, just as every soccer referee has his own priorities.

Offsides in front of the goal are beyond comprehension

SINCE it involves a lot of "iffy" situations, I had doubts about even including it. I am doing so for the obvious reason that what happens in front of the goal is critical, and it's where (c), "the ball last touched by an opponent, or was last played by him (the shooter)" most often applies.

Skipping the obvious, like a pass to a forward all alone in front of the goal, and offside for all the world to see, let's try to clarify things by examples of less-obvious, but quite common situations.

Fig. 1. On a corner-kick, Player A positions himself right on the goal line. If the ball comes to him directly, untouched by anyone else on his team, his goal counts, because the offside rule doesn't apply to corner-kicks. If he deflects the ball, on purpose or accidentally, to Player B who scores, it does not count, because once someone touches a corner-kick it's no longer a corner-kick, and A is offside.

Fig. 2. Player A is not offside because he has received the direct from a goal-kick. If the ball had reached Player B first, then A would have been offside. Similarly, A would have played himself offside by passing *back* to B. His best bet would have been to try a shot at goal.

Fig. 3. Player A shoots on goal, and hits an upright, or the crossbar. The ball rebounds to him, and he kicks, or heads it, into the net. The goal counts, because he himself last played the ball.

Fig. 4. The ball rebounds to Player B who converts it. Now the goal doesn't count, because B didn't play the ball last, and A is offside.

Fig. 5. Instead of a yes/no ruling, it becomes a yes/yes ruling if the keeper deflects the shot taken by Player A. If A knocks the deflect into the goal it counts, because the ball was last touched by an opponent. If Player B scores off the keeper deflect, even though A is now offside it still counts for the same reason unless Player A interferes with the keeper.

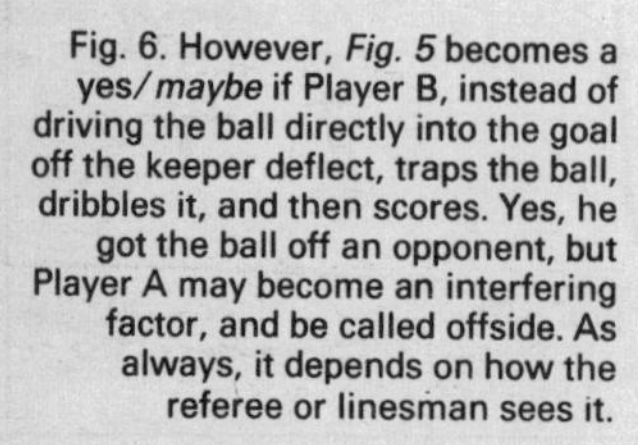

Fig. 6. However, *Fig. 5* becomes a yes/*maybe* if Player B, instead of driving the ball directly into the goal off the keeper deflect, traps the ball, dribbles it, and then scores. Yes, he got the ball off an opponent, but Player A may become an interfering factor, and be called offside. As always, it depends on how the referee or linesman sees it.

Messy, isn't it? At that, these are the easier, more clear-cut examples. It can get like a pinball game in front of the goal, and there's really no way an offensive player can protect himself from being caught momentarily out of position. Or, as you can imagine, for officials to always get things right.

For spectators it's frustrating to watch the ball thundered into the net only to have the goal negated. But, is it any more so than having a touchdown called back for an offside that might have had no influence whatsoever?

Well, back in the formative years of soccer rules, those perceptive lads had taken that into account having enabled the referee to ignore an offside if he had felt that it had not been a factor in a play. More than enable, the wording is that a player "shall not" be whistled offside unless he *is* a factor — "interfering with the play or with an opponent, or is seeking to gain an advantage by being in an offside position."

Even though the player in the dark shirt (arrowed) has not got the ball, he is in an offside position but the referee and linesman consider that he is interfering with play and award an indirect free-kick to the opposition.

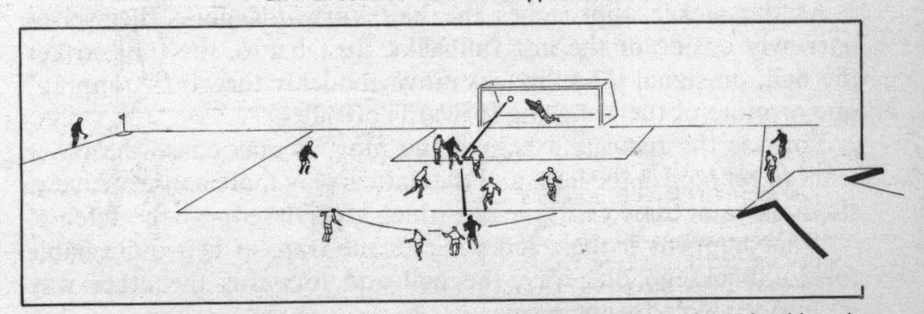

This time the player is not considered to be interfering with play. The goal stands, although, again, the interpretation rests with the officials on what constitutes interfering and not interfering. Another referee might still have given a free-kick.

To cite a clearcut situation, the attack is coming along the left sideline, and the right wing is a couple of yards ahead of the ball across the field. He's at least 50 yards away, and hardly a participant in the play. But, what if he cuts towards the middle while still offside? At some point — and it's up to the referee to decide — he becomes a potential factor, most likely drawing a defender away from the action, and should be called.

To muddy the waters even more, once offside and a factor, a player can't move back onside and start over. The best he can do is take himself out of the play in some obvious manner, like squatting to retie a shoelace, or falling flat on his face.

Now put yourself in his position. When does he become a whistleable factor? He hasn't been called so far, and might not be. Should he continue in hopes of helping score a goal, and risk seeing it nullified?

Taking himself out of the play would be a shrewd act by Player A in Fig. 6 above, so a goal scored by B would be allowed. Okay so far, but what happens if the keeper now deflects B's shot right on to A's foot? If I were A, then I would go ahead and score, keeping myself as unobtrusive as possible, and letting the officials worry about it. What's to be lost anyway?

The Offside Trap

BEFORE leaving the offside rule, we should take a moment to analyze a tactic some teams use to draw the other team offside, usually on free-kicks.

As the kicker approaches the ball, forwards poise themselves narrowly onside of the last fullbacks. Just before the foot strikes the ball, on signal the fullbacks move suddenly forward "trapping" one or more of the opposing forwards offside.

You see the reasoning behind the ploy. It may cause the other team to relinquish the ball, and thereafter, play more conservatively, staying two or three yards onside, which gives the edge to the defense.

What happens if the referee misses the trap, as he's quite liable to? Fullbacks go one way, the ball and forwards the other way . . .hysteria time for the keeper.

The Offside Trap works fine when with qualified linesmen, but it's dangerous with just one decision-making official.

Now for that notorious twelfth rule . . .

AS the offside rule sets the stage for team soccer, Rule 12 defines individual soccer. It tells us how the one-on-one confrontations must be conducted, which is vital, since bodies often collide at full speed. Determining whether an infraction is "intentional," and major or minor, would stretch the judicial capabilities of the Supreme Court.

A rule of thumb, or toe if you insist, is that bumping while in pursuit of a ball is inevitable, and therefore, legal. In other circumstances, the "ball first" mandate prevails.

Major infractions calling for a direct free-kick — meaning if the ball goes in the goal untouched by another player it counts — result from most forms of *intentional* collision where the body, rather than the ball, is the target . . .kicking, tripping, hitting, holding, for example.

Included as a major infraction is "hands" — striking the ball with hand or arm (below shoulder). If unintentional, as it usually is, a penalty should not be called, however, there's an interpretation not mentioned by the rule-makers, but usually applied by referees. *Even when unintentional, like a hard kick at short range hitting a player on the arm, if the result is a significant advantage for that player's team, a penalty may be called.*

Minor infractions are essentially scaled-down versions of major infractions, like: a legal charge, with the shoulder, but when the ball is elsewhere on the field; obstructing an opponent in what amounts to a "pick" play; or trying to kick the ball out of the hands of the goalkeeper when, in the referee's opinion, the keeper had "possession."

Included among minor infractions is a vague reference to "dangerous play." Most are high kicks in close proximity to another player (obviously another judgment call).

Rule #12 also has a lot to say about a player's conduct on the field, both in regard to opponents and officials. If, in the opinion of the referee, a player "is guilty of violent conduct or serious foul play," or uses "foul or abusive language," he will get a warning. The same is true if he persists in hassling the referee over a call.

Play will be stopped, a yellow card waved in his face, and the ball awarded the other team for an indirect free-kick. The second time, he's likely to get a red card, and be removed from the game. A "red-carded" player cannot be replaced by a substitute, so his team plays the rest of the game short-handed, and he's barred from playing in the next game.

Not a bad idea, is it? This keeps the game on course, and dispositions under tight rein. The keep-your-mouth-shut rule also, and especially, applies to coaches. (In my 15th year of coaching, I finally got a red card myself for making a sarcastic comment to the referee after a game — and I deserved it.)

What we have, under terms of Rule #12, is what amounts to a contact/non-contact sport, not unlike what we're seeing these days on a basketball court. We'll probe this after we complete the basic rules.

The "restart" rules and we're done . . .Momentarily

ALTHOUGH the various restarts provide opportunities for set plays, at this juncture we'll limit ourselves to the rules themselves.

It figures that right after Rule #12 would come the punishments for the crimes — free-kicks, direct for major crimes, and indirect for all others. The difference is what the names imply. A **Direct Free-Kick** can score directly without touching anyone else. An **Indirect Free-Kick** has to touch, or be touched, by someone else before a goal can be scored. Who and which team provides the "second touch" doesn't matter, as long as it isn't the person who kicked it originally, which is why I mentioned earlier that many goals are scored off unsuspecting rear ends.

For all free-kicks, nobody on the offending team can be within 10 yards of the ball *until it is kicked.* Sometimes players react to the referee's whistle, rather than the contact with the ball, in which case the offended team can take the kick again.

*The **Penalty Kick** is a special, and to my mind, barbaric case of the direct free-kick.* It is awarded when a defender commits a major infraction within the penalty area, and I suppose, could be termed the ultimate shoot-out — kicker versus goalkeeper at point-blank, 12-yard range — except that the keeper has no weapon. The odds heavily favor the kicker, which is appropriate, in that the foul probably prevented a pretty good shot, and inappropriate, in that the keeper probably wasn't at fault.

A few other points about the penalty-kick. Any player can take the kick, and teams have players so designated for reasons we'll

When stationing defenders in a wall ten yards from the ball on free-kicks within scoring range, the keeper should make sure that it extends beyond the upright away from where he stations himself. This is to prevent a skilled kicker "bending" the ball around the wall. A Pelé, for instance, might sneak the ball into that gap on the right-hand side here. Incidentally, the wallers aren't adjusting their underwear. Men can protect their lower parts just as woman their upper parts — as long as they don't use their hands or arms for other than self-protective purposes.

The classic confrontation — penalty-taker against goalkeeper. The kicker will be feeling the pressure. The keeper probably feels that he is in a no-win situation.

Goalkeeper's view of a defensive wall. Often he won't see the ball until it flashes around those defenders.

The main problem at a throw-in is to find someone to throw *to.* In the top inset, the thrower-in has to throw to a colleague who is tightly marked. In the lower inset, a fellow player has run into space, although that's difficult to find in such a situation. Incidentally, the thrower-in cannot throw to himself.

delve into later. The keeper cannot move until the ball is kicked. Other players on the kicker's team have to remain the usual 10 yards away until contact is made with the ball.

If the ball clangs back off the upright or crossbar, it can be fired again by anyone other than the kicker. However, if the keeper deflects the ball, it's fair game for everyone.

A Throw-In *is taken by the team that does not touch the ball last before it passes completely over the sideline, or is taken against* *the team that does touch the ball last* — whichever makes more sense to you.

I've always wondered who made up the throw-in rule (#15), but he must have been a misanthrope or a contortionist. For me, it's an entirely unnatural action. Maybe he was a she, because some women with less than half my upper body strength can throw the ball more than twice as far. It's all in the technique: face the field, take the ball in both hands back behind your head, and whip the ball forward with arms extended, but without imparting any spin, lifting a foot off the ground, crossing the line, or twisting the body. If you want to switch, and throw to a different player, you have to reposition your body to face his way. (See what I mean about "unnatural?" It's my only solace.)

The ***Goal-Kick*** *is a restart when an attacking team last touches the ball before it crosses the endline.* Placing the ball on the corner of the goal area, on the side the ball went out of bounds, a defender kicks it upfield. No one on the other team can be within the penalty area, or for that matter, touch the ball until it crosses that 18-yard line. If it fails to cross the line, the kick is retaken. Once beyond the penalty area, it's in play. Needless to say, attackers like to lurk out there, since an errant goal-kick is a sitting duck.

Not a common occurance in top-class soccer, but further down the ladder, there is always the chance of receiving a scoring chance direct from a goal-kick when the keeper miskicks. Once the ball is outside the penalty area, the lucky forward (who's onside, remember) can have a shot.

The goal-kick is an indirect, which is a *non sequitor* anyway, since it's hardly likely to travel the length of the field, and into the other goal, untouched by someone along the way.

By this time, you'll realize that the goal-kick is an exception to the rule about opposing players remaining 10 yards away. Since the goal area extends 6 yards out, and the penalty area 18 yards out, opposing players are actually *12* yards away when the ball is kicked.

The final rule covers the **Corner-Kick** *which comes about if the defending team last touched the ball before it crossed the endline.* Placed down within that one-yard arc by the corner-flag, the ball is put back in play by the attacking team. The set-play possibilities are endless, including, since it's a *direct* free-kick, a skilled player curving the ball into the goal from that corner-arc. We'll discuss these later.

By keeping the rules and wordage limited, the International Board left room for evolutionary improvements after thorough testing. Unlike some of our sports, where rules are yanked back and forth, almost annually, far from the playing fields, the future of soccer is on the feet of the players.

Soccer Is A Contact/Non-Contact Sport

WHAT I mean by this apparent contradiction is that there is plenty of physical contact on a soccer field, although the rules prohibit contact, except within carefully-defined limits. *No contact is allowed unless players are going for the ball!* Basketball is also a contradiction, and we're seeing what can happen as larger, stronger people participate.

There's no such contradiction with football, rugby, and hockey. They are contact/contact sports. The rules allow body contact — insist upon it! — no matter where the ball or puck may be. And, that's the way these games are played. (Field hockey is an example of the other extreme — non-contact/non-contact.)

Soccer should be a *finesse* sport played aggressively with technical (individual), and tactical (team) skills employed, with purposeful or incidental contact. But the reality is that overaggression often pays off.

The rules of soccer emphasize that the ball, rather than the body, is the primary target. A worthy theory, yet the actuality is, that when two players charge at a ball, they are likely to have contact. And, the player who does *not* pull up wins.

You know the saying — "Rugby is a ruffians' sport played by gentlemen; soccer is a gentlemen's sport played by ruffians." Less a matter of who then *why*. By being an outright contact/contact without protective garb, players get all the physicality they could want or endure. As such, there's also a built-in control mechanism which is, in effect, self-preservation. *Don't do unto others lest they do unto you.*

A contact/non-contact sport has no such control mechanism beyond what the coaches, officials, and especially the players instill, and what spectators come to appreciate.

The rules of soccer, by telling you what *not* to do, imply that anything and everything else is "fair game." Eliminate the negative

Sliding tackles can be dangerous in the penalty area. In A the defender has got to the ball first and that's a fair tackle. In B, too, the referee might feel that a fair challenge was made. In C the defender has already pushed the ball away and even though the attacker falls over his outstretched leg, it isn't a foul.

and accentuate the positive, to adapt an old Cole Porter ditty. Examine what is *not* allowed to determine what *is* allowed. The implied intent, *that generally if the ball is struck first, whatever follows is okay,* leads to problems of interpretation.

For instance, when two players are running side-by-side in pursuit of a ball, a "shoulder-charge" is allowed. Each can try to shoulder (not elbow) the other off the ball. However, charging from behind with the shoulder is a major infraction. Shoving sideways or shoving forward — it's a fine line.

When a lofted pass is coming down, two players may jump to head the ball. Each has the right to gain position by shouldering the other, yet it's an illegal tactic when one player knocks the other too soon, or too late . . .another fine line.

Tripping an opponent is a no-no in Rule 12, yet in a legal slide tackle the player tackled is likely to be tripped up. Was the ball

It's OK to shoulder-charge each other, providing that those elbows are tucked in.

struck first? If so, it should be legal. But, what if the tackler "accidentally" upends the opponent after striking the ball? . . .or if the annoyed tackler just happens to tramp on the tackler while he's in such an inviting, and vulnerable position on the ground?

And where's the dividing line between capitalizing on a goalkeeper's fumble, and creating a dangerous play? . . .or the keeper using his rights of protection to sideswipe a charging forward?

Larger fields are the best finesse reponse

WATCHING televised soccer from Europe, you may wonder why a player moving with the ball is allowed so much freedom . . .why defenders tend to back-off to shepherd, and cover, rather than attack. It's because, *on a full-scale field,* finesse prevails over aggression.

A skilled player in possession of the ball can maneuver with it, or pass accurately in a split-second. For an opponent more than two or three yards away to charge, is to invite disaster, and embarrassment.

However, on a small field — yes, I'm bemoaning football fields again — the players are crammed in closer together, so it's more likely someone will be close enough to make that charge. The result is destructive, rather than constructive soccer — get rid of the ball fast, rather than take time to set something up.

It's much the same thing in hockey. Hockey rinks are too small. If they played on larger, European-sized rinks, we'd see more Gretzkys, and more finesse.

The fact that basketball instituted the three-point rule suggests they'd like more finesse, and less under-the-basket mayhem. *Both sports would benefit from larger playing surfaces, but can't do much about it . . .soccer can and should.*

What The Referee Has To Cope With

THEORETICALLY, according to Rules 5 and 6, three officials — a referee and two linesmen — govern a soccer game, but once the fracas begins, near-total responsibility rests on the shoulders of the referee, who is the official on the field . . .the *only* official on the field!

He is in command "as soon as he enters the field of play," and he can even remove a linesman who displeases him. (I doubt it happens often, but can you conceive of a football referee ejecting a backfield judge, or a home plate umpire chasing his buddy away from first base?) Yet, it all comes together and makes sense in soccer's own unique context.

How three qualified officials coordinate is rather interesting, and may not be immediately apparent.

Each linesman ranges his sideline (touchline) staying pretty much in one half, so he can also cover his goal line (endline) to signal when the ball goes out of bounds . . .totally over the line . . .and which team has possession at the restart. He also signals offsides, and any foul the referee may not see, although the referee may choose to ignore the flag, and let play continue.

Rather than have to dash around trying to be everywhere at once, now the referee can move diagonally from corner to corner at a more measured pace. This enables him to stay close to the action, and make out of bounds calls beyond the view of the linesmen. Another feature of the diagonal system is that referee and linesman now have different perspectives of action in front of the goal.

It's worth saying again that, in soccer, a foul isn't a foul unless the referee says it is. A violation of rules is ignored unless, in his sole opinion, it constitutes unsportsmanlike or dangerous conduct, or alters the course of play in favor of the offending team.

If not busy enough controlling 22 people running madly around a near-two-acre plot of turf for 90 minutes, the referee keeps the score, the record of infractions, and even the official time. If there's a stadium clock, it operates by guesswork, because the referee may add extra time to make up for unusual delays — and only he knows how much.

Thus, the referee is blessed, and at the same time cursed, with an unparalled degree of latitude. (Don't you wonder what he does out there with all his spare time?)

Look at the nature of the game in relation to the officiating structure. Having several officials, each with a different responsibility, makes sense in football, because every play is a separate (albeit perfunctory) event, and players themselves have different responsibilities with different rules. No single referee could do it all. Furthermore, the ball is dead between plays, and at a restart, players are in definable areas, so the zebras (and the omnipotent reviewers) can confer at will — and mind-numbing length.

In soccer, all field players function the same way with the same rules. The ball is only dead when the whistle blows, and players may be anywhere at restarts. Therefore, right or wrong, decisions have to be made instantly. There's no time to powwow.

What may now occur to you is that if there *are* three qualified officials, they can be better employed without altering the basic structure. Why not have two referees, each responsible for half the field — a much more manageable task — and the third, like the table-jockeys beside a basketball court, tracking the score, time, infractions, substitutes, and stray dogs?

The two-referee system is sometimes used, and it certainly helps when the referees aren't in condition to cover the entire field effectively. The problem rests with that a-foul-may-not-be-a-foul rule. Players need to have a consistent policy as to what they can and cannot get away with. No doubt two referees would have different priorities, which would cause confusion and controversy. It would be like having two umpires behind the plate on alternate innings.

The referee's job is to let the players play

THAT, patient people, is the gist of it. Rather than being an intrusive element, as we're accustomed to — "hogging the spotlight" in some cases — the referee is a part of the game. *In fact, if the ball strikes him, it's still in play.* His job is to stay out of the way, and only interfere when necessary.

Looking at it another way, football at its best gives us maybe 15 minutes of action over a three-hour time span. With everything decided instantly, consistently, and with no discussions or arguments, soccer gives us about 60 minutes of action in less than two hours, including half-time.

Controlling the intimidation factor early on

NOW, having just said that a referee should be on the scene, yet not seen, in the early minutes he may be quite in evidence making a few dubious calls, especially involving the two most essential rules — offsides and personal fouls. He knows that to *maintain* control, he first has to *establish* control.

By being a "quick whistle" in the beginning, and with impartiality, even if he has to bend the rules a tad, he notifies everyone he's going to call a tight game as most better teams prefer. If he's too casual during the opening minutes, players will get the message, and the game will get out of hand.

Being a contact/non-contact sport, intimidation plays a major role in soccer. Establishing your turf, and getting space to operate in, is part of the game. But, lesser teams may try to make up for their talent shortcomings by physical means, by stretching the rules to whatever limits a referee will permit, and they are sure to test his limits early on.

Parallels between soccer fouls and football interference

THERE surely are other parallels, but the rules governing interference in football come to mind immediately.

In both sports, players moving into position to receive a pass are supposed to have an unobstructed pathway until the ball approaches, at which time it's up for grabs. And, at that time, interference can be called either way, since both attacker and defender are allowed equal access to the ball. When two players are contesting for the ball, collisions are inevitable, and accepted as long as they

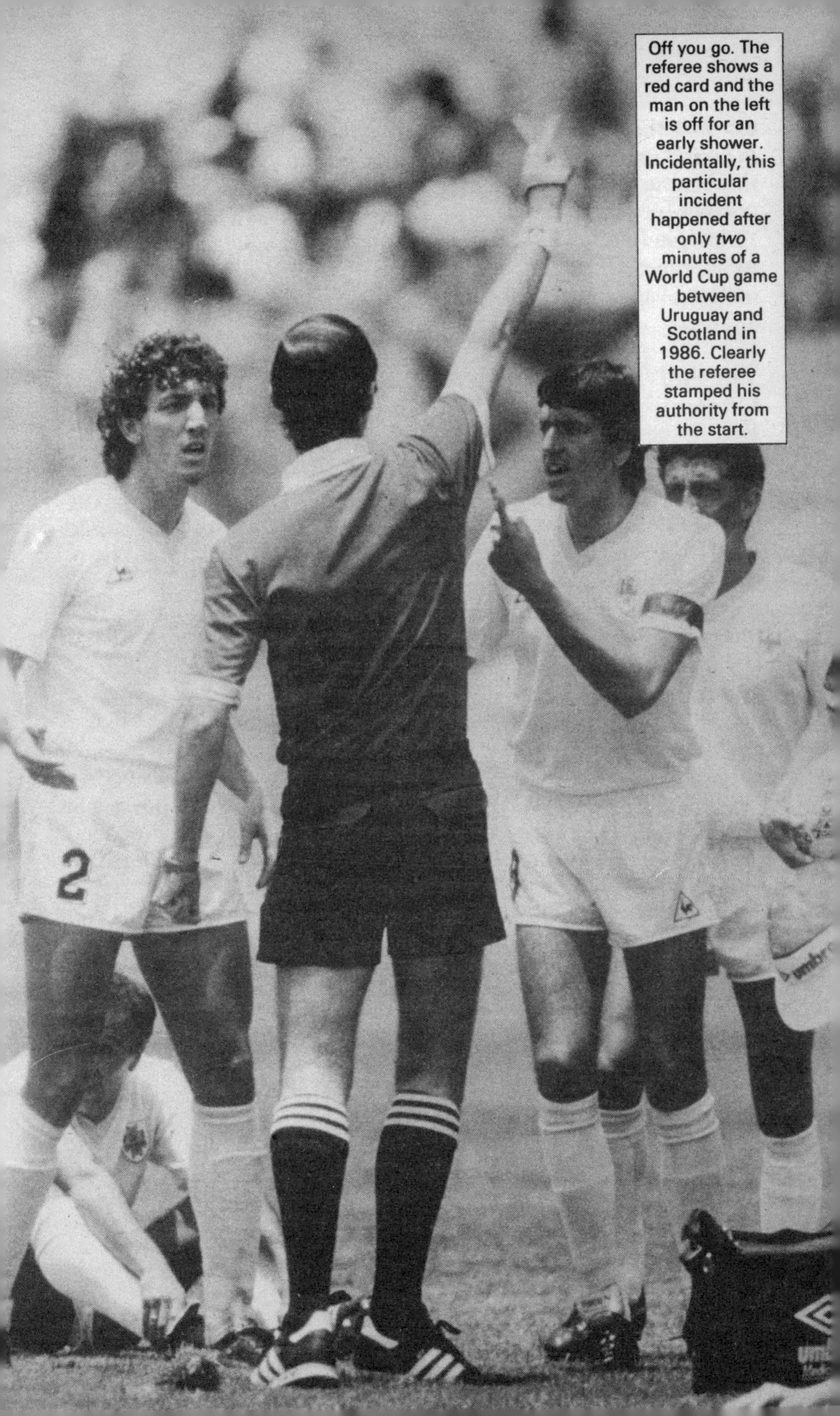

Off you go. The referee shows a red card and the man on the left is off for an early shower. Incidentally, this particular incident happened after only *two* minutes of a World Cup game between Uruguay and Scotland in 1986. Clearly the referee stamped his authority from the start.

are within reason, and the target is the ball rather than the body. Whoever gains possession, the other player must try to tackle — that's also the word in soccer — to regain possession, or at least prevent further progress.

And, in football as in soccer, interference is a judgment call made by a single official. If one player is fouled, yet ends up with the ball, the "advantage" rule prevails.

The "advantage" rule is the toughest call of all

YOU'D be correct in reminding me that the advantage rule always applies in football, since the referee can "refuse" the offended team any free-kick if he thinks it's to their advantage to do so. *But, the soccer official, by making the call, is also making the decision.* If he blows it, there's no way he can unblow it, figuratively as well as literally.

Rule 5 includes this clause: "He shall refrain from penalizing in all cases where he is satisfied that, by so doing, he would be giving the advantage to the offending team."

If you read this clause carefully, you'll understand that the referee not only may decline to call a penalty, he *must* decline if he figures the advantage would go the wrong way.

But, how can he be "satisfied" at the moment the foul occurs? He may call a foul just before the ball ends up in the possession of the offended team, and inadvertently benefit the offending team by saving them from a threatening situation, and enabling them to regroup before the free-kick.

And, even if the offended team does retain possession, the foul may be so flagrant that the referee cannot ignore it. Intent is always a major determinant, and, this again, is in the eye of the black-clothed beholder.

Reluctance to call "majors" in the penalty area

THERE'S a collision just within the penalty area, and the referee calls a foul on the fullback responsible. Diverting everyone's attention to a passing nuclear missile, he steps back and places the ball just *outside* the line.

Hey, what is this? Why isn't it a penalty-kick? . . .because referees are reluctant to award penalty-kicks. It's almost a sure goal for the other side, and the foul itself may be less flagrant than others should be determined by merit.

If the foul is intentional and occurs well inside the area, that's a different matter. Since the foul was perpetrated to prevent a shot being taken, and without regard for injury to the attacker, a penalty-kick is appropriate. If not intentional and close to the border, though, you may see him move the ball just beyond the penalty area. Being a direct kick at short range, it's still dangerous, but now the defending team can assist the goalkeeper by forming a wall in front of the goal.

On the other hand, a referee is not reluctant at all to call major fouls outside the penalty area, because they are often very deliberate as well as dangerous.

If an attacker eludes a defender, and has a clear pathway to a shooting spot, the defender may try to flatten him from behind before he reaches the penalty area. Many coaches make it part of their game plan, since it's almost a no-lose maneuver. If successful, the fouler disrupts what could be a point-blank shot on goal. The action itself, being obvious, may draw a "quick whistle," which stops the threat and thwarts the advantage rule.

You can appreciate the referee's dilemma in such situations. By calling a foul outside the penalty area, he may be giving the advantage to the *offending* team. By *not* calling the penalty, he may seem to condone unsportsmanlike conduct and lose control.

What he hopes is that the defender will fail so that he can let play continue. Better yet, if the defender goes too far, and commits the foul *inside* the penalty area, the referee can nail him and award a penalty-kick from that 12-yard spot.

Protecting the goalkeeper

AWARE that the goalkeeper, like a kicker in football, is vulnerable the moment he gets his hands on the ball, especially when on the ground, referees tend to be almost over-protective. Rule 12 prohibits an attacker from colliding with the keeper before or while he's going for the ball which is pretty clear-cut, but prohibiting an attacker from "attempting to kick the ball while held by the goalkeeper" is another judgment situation.

Your interpretation of "held" is as good as anyone else's. Given that fouling the keeper is a minor risk, who can blame a forward for trying to kick it out of his hands? Referees tend to be over-protective of keepers just for that reason. Should a sterner penalty be exacted? I certainly think so!

"Whattya mean offside . . .!"

JUST a reminder that you better get used to most dubious offsides calls being made in favor of the defense. In the confusion in front of the goal we can tolerate dubious calls, because we can't be sure ourselves, but it's frustrating further upfield when we can see that our player was distinctly onside when the ball was played.

It's simply a matter of one set of eyes being unable to see everything at the same time. During a free-kick, the referee can move down, and station himself in line with the last fullback, but otherwise he has to focus on the action, and depend on peripheral vision to spot the relationship of attackers and defenders. If unsure, he figures it's better to call a halt than allow what might result in an undeserved score.

Forget about your democratic right to dissent

UNDER Rule 12 the referee has the obligation to prevent "ungentlemanly conduct," especially "violent conduct or serious foul play," and the right to stomp on any expression of displeasure as to his calls.

The first time is liable to be a yellow card flashed in the culprit's face, and a direct free-kick for the other team. Do it again, and it's a red card, which means that the player is gone for the rest of the game, and probably the next. Since that player cannot be replaced, his team plays short-footed thereafter.

Referees can even call a game for "interference by spectators." It seldom happens, but be aware that the Benevolent Dictator has the right to forfeit a game if people along the sidelines persist in yammering at him. More likely, he'll treat a loud-mouth sideliner like a misbehaving player — yellow card meaning shut up, red card meaning go home.

The coach is responsible for his spectators. More than once I've clamped the lid on a parental sideliner before the referee had to, or became so annoyed he'd retaliate in his calls.

No-one knows better than the referee when he's made a bum call, and if a bit unsure of himself, he's likely to be sensitive about it. If people hoot and holler at him, he'll overreact, and start throwing cards around in an attempt to reestablish his authority. Keep on his case, and your team won't get a favorable call the rest of the way.

Keep your mouth shut, and he'll probably try to balance things out with a later call. Besides, your team will get the same referee again, and he may have a long memory.

Arm up, arm pointing . . .that's it for referee signals

WHEN the referee whistles a foul, and raises his arm straight up, it's a minor, which means an indirect free-kick. When he points

The referee (left) points towards the goal of the offending team to indicate a direct (major) free-kick. The referee on the right is raising his arm high to signal an indirect free-kick.

To foul or not to foul? These players will probably get away with high kicking but if there had been an opponent's head in the way, then dangerous play would have been called.

towards the goal of the offending team, it's a major, and a *direct* free-kick. Just as there are only two rules that govern play, there are just these two simple signals that govern restarts, and herein lies a potential quandary.

Which signal did he give? Since there isn't much difference, and there's no loudspeaker system attached to the referee, players may be unsure. If doubt exists, it's up to the team captains to make sure and spread the word.

There is a movement afoot, in this country, to have referees use a wider range of signals, comparable to football, mostly for the benefit of spectators. The trouble is, it would take all kinds of theatrics and athleticism to differentiate among obstruction, holding, tripping, charging, jumping in, pushing, hands, etc. Referees would need ballet training to express a "high kick." (Hands over ears to indicate "foul or abusive language?" Somehow I just can't see it happening.)

By this time you should anticipate a more important reason why soccer referees will probably stick to simple traditions. There's a saying that sums up what we've seen about the role of the referee in soccer. *If he comes off the field without anyone being aware he was even out there, he's called a good game.* The fewer gyrations the better. (Just watch me be proved wrong!)

All You Need To Know About Formations

AH, at last Cook, you're getting around to formations. What took you so long? How can one really understand what's going on out there without a thorough grasp of formations?

If your life does indeed depend on understanding the origins, evolutions, and intricacies of the 4-3-3, 4-4-2, 4-2-4, etc., there are how-to texts. However, texts written or updated more recently — *and by coaches with experience in this country* — downplay formations, because they don't mean as much in modern free-wheeling soccer. Once the game starts, everything changes. That's the essence of soccer, after all.

Graham Ramsay, the Britisher, who has done so much to educate young American soccer players, cautions that soccer formations should only be considered "patterns" or "frameworks." He objects to the very word "formation," because it implies feet-cast-in-concrete inflexibility. It also implies that soccer could develop football-like set plays, if only coaches and players would forget all the free-wheeling stuff, and put their minds to it.

Walt Chyzowych, former U.S. National Coach and Director of Coaching for the United States Soccer Federation, concurs, and suggests the phrase "systems of play," and I admit it's kind of catchy. In *THE OFFICIAL SOCCER BOOK OF THE UNITED STATES SOCCER FEDERATION* (Eastwood Printing & Publishing), he devotes only eight out of 270 pages to the topic of formations, which is a pretty good tip-off in itself, and why my own chapter on the subject will be brief.

The Rule of Ten

ASSUMING the goalkeeper is in or near the goal, soccer formations add up to ten by threes, signifying defense, midfield, and offense, in that order. And, since ten isn't divisible by three, defense, midfield, and offense cannot, of course, be equally structured.

Thus, the popular 4-3-3 formation has four defenders, three midfielders, and three attackers. They're designated, you'll recall, as a sweeper nearest the goal, two wing or outside fullbacks, and a (forward) stopper — the midfield as left, center, and right halfbacks (or just midfielders) — and the offense as left and right wings, and the center-forward in the middle.

The 3-3-4 is the flip-side of the 4-3-3 with one less defender and one more attacker. The 4-4-2, with its four fullbacks, and an equal number of halfbacks, seems paranoid about the other team setting up camp at midfield. The 4-2-4 seems schizophrenic, unable to decide whether to attack or defend, although the Brazilians used it to brilliant effect some years ago. But, in soccer, seeming is deceiving, and all formations have their origins and purposes usually linked to the talent available.

Because you may hear reference to defensive, midfield, or offensive "lines," in my diagrams I show players in approximate freeze-action positions, to emphasize that the idea of any or no formation is to cover the field — *in depth, width, and time.*

One exception to the numbering system is the "WM," so-named because three fullbacks and two defense halfbacks form a "W" when seen from that hovering blimp, and three forwards and two offensive halfbacks form an "M." I know, flip it around and it's an "MW," except it isn't, because formation designations start with the defense. I know, too, it could fit the numbering criterion as a 3-4-3, only it doesn't function as a 3-4-3. At least it didn't originally, because it was designed with five man-on-man defenders, as in a 5-2-3.

Although it's useful for beginning teams, you seldom see the "WM" today, because it represented defensive overkill, which the fans didn't like, and, anyway, the Brazilians, with Pelé, blew it away in the 1958 World Cup.

A fascinating aspect of sports is that one individual can change the nature of formations. Every year some track star would take a fling at the NFL, touted to be an undefendable wide receiver, only to prove to be undependable, because he couldn't hang on to the ball in traffic. Then along came Bob Hayes.

Because Hayes had played football in college, he could not only outsprint any single defender, but could also catch the ball afterwards, and be gone. Football defenses had to adapt with the zone defense, and disguised double coverage. Not all by himself, nor perhaps even the first, Pelé, nevertheless, gets credit for altering the traditional man-on-man coverage, as in the "WM."

The Student-Body-Charge Era

WE'VE talked a lot about the impact of the pass on soccer, but nothing illustrates it more dramatically, than the first official international soccer-football game in 1872, between Scotland and England. In those days, soccer players didn't *pass* the ball — they simply dribbled with it towards the opposing goal, until they were robbed by a crowd of defenders. You can imagine what happened. Like tots on the pitch today, everyone chased whoever had the ball. The players, not being tot-sized, it must have reflected the mayhem deplored by earlier monarchs.)

The Scots used a 2-2-6 formation, and the Brits actually played 1-1-8 — *fourteen* forwards on the field, and they couldn't score a single goal amongst them. (I don't know how long they played headless chicken, but they probably called it quits from sheer exhaustion and frustration.)

The Scots themselves are given credit for introducing the passing game, but it would have happened anyway. Sooner or later, the dribbler would have put the ball too far ahead, and on to the foot of a mate, who would have figured, "since the ball's right here, why not keep it going as long as nobody blows a whistle." (In those days two umpires controlled the game and the referee was only called in to rule on disputes, when the umpires — one from each side — couldn't agree).

You can say that the pass actually created formations as we now know them. Since a kicked ball travels faster than people can run, players have to be disbursed around the field. It also brought about the offside rule, to prevent an enemy agent from lurking in the goalkeeper's doorway.

Availability of talent influences formations

THE selection of formations depends on the players a coach has to work with. In fact, that's how most formations came into being in the first place. The trouble is, whatever seems to work is often mimicked by other coaches, without regard to their own talent pool . . .sound familiar?

To give you an extreme example, the Italians lost 17 of their best national players in a 1949 plane crash. Their only chance with lesser talent was to keep *eight* players hanging back, hoping to shut the other teams out, and for a lucky break by the three offensive players. It was named the *catenaccio*, and introduced the "free-back" (sweeper or *libero* in more recent parlance), who roamed behind other defenders picking up anyone breaking through. While the free-back concept remains, the *catenaccio* itself faded away, because it was too defensive.

Then, in the 1958 World Cup, along came that now-famous Brazilian team with a forward named Pelé, and another scoring threat, if less renowned, named Vava. To make the most of both, the Brazilians concocted a 4-2-4, which quickly became the accepted pattern for many other national teams in the 1960s. For a while, defense took a back seat to offense.

Sir Alfred Ramsey, the English national coach in the late 1960s, found he had too much talent in the midfield, and not enough at the wings to use the 4-3-3, so he devised a system with four defenders, four midfielders, two forwards — and no wings, as such. Inadvertently, he enabled defense to climb over into the front seat, take the wheel, and, in effect, shoved offense out the door.

Having that extra midfielder gave them unusual flexibility, and the element of surprise. One of the two forwards might angle towards the corner with one or more midfielders advancing into the striker position, or an outside halfback might sprint along the sidelines to act as wing. Either way, the novelty must have caused defenders to run into each other trying to figure out who covered who.

Creating confusion is always the objective, whatever the formation, because mistakes cause goals in any team sport.

Since Ramsey's English team won a world championship with his *ad hoc* formation, other teams caught the wingless bug, only they often carried his 4-4-2 to a 5-5-1 defensive extreme — sometimes a 10-0-0 — on the premise that if the other team can't score, we can't lose . . .(shades of George Allen?). However, if everyone does it, nobody can *win*, either. So, soccer in the 1970's went through a scoring drought until, as attendance at games dropped sharply, coaches came to their (fiscal) senses.

Once play starts, formations can sometimes become jumbled. These players are taking part in the 1983 World Youth Tournament between Argentina and China.

If they did — and do — employ the 4-4-2, it's with Sir Alfred's original purpose of creating a multiple offense, where any of three or four players can become wings. We'll see how in a moment.

Why the 4-3-3 is the most popular formation

YOU'LL see the 4-3-3 most frequently, because it's best-suited for teams with varied talent. It has four defenders, and makes best use of the other six field players, without placing undue demands upon them. With a sweeper, stopper and center-half, it has solid

Locate the goalkeeper (top of the picture) and you'll find everyone else — four defenders, three midfielders and three strikers up front.

"strength up the middle." It features balance between offense and defense, which characterizes modern soccer.

To better appreciate the logic of the 4-3-3, compare it with the 4-2-4, which embodies an extra attacker at the expense of the center-half. Since two midfielders will frequently be over-matched, one of the forwards, often the left wing, has to drop back to help.

I'd rather have three players in the midfield, and have one of them move up to support the three forwards. Moving *up* is preferable to moving *back* for a couple of reasons. First, the midfielder has a better view of the action in front of him, and can move in that direction more effectively. Second, failure to move up is less self-destructive than failure to move back.

Furthermore, in addition to eliminating the center-half, who is a uniquely vital operative, the 4-2-4 eliminates both the sweeper and stopper, who are equally vital to the defense. Yes, there are still four fullbacks, but they don't provide the depth of the 4-3-3 to deal with a dangerous center-forward. If he gets by the stopper, he's vulnerable to the sweeper, because dribbling is an *ahead* maneuver. For that reason, it's easier to fake out two inside fullbacks approaching from opposite sides. (Probably they assume stopper and sweeper roles anyway, so why not set things up that way?)

On the other hand, the 4-4-2 overstocks the midfield, so to generate threats, halfbacks have to become forwards. Moving up may be preferable to moving back, but this represents a lot of extra sprinting, and the likelihood of lost opportunities. Then too, those four people in the midfield have to function well together, otherwise they get in each other's way. *Three's company, four's a crowd.*

Certainly more logical than the 4-2-4, the 4-4-2 still calls for more talent, coordination, and endurance, than the 4-3-3.

The 3-3-4 – when you really need a goal

ALTHOUGH it's risky having only three designated defenders, a team may switch to this formation if they are behind late in the game. Unless you're in a tournament where the goals differential matters, losing is losing, so why not go for it?

In effect, the formation is swung 180 degrees, so that the offense, rather than the defense, forms a diamond pattern. What was the stopper becomes what I call a "trailing forward" operating five to ten yards behind the center-forward/striker. (The sweeper then becomes a center fullback.)

Being beyond the turmoil, in front of the goal, this player can find open space in which to receive passes, and redirect loose balls weakly cleared by the defense. If you've noticed the tendency of teams in the lead to pull back their defense and jam the goalmouth, you'll realize how hard it is for a forward to score, even with a quality shot. There are too many bodies in the way.

The 3-3-4 partly alleviates this problem. Being further back, the trailing forward can shoot over the heads of the amassed bodies, and perhaps find an upper corner of the goal beyond the reach

A defender has been sacrificed in order to have an extra forward in this 3-3-4 formation. The problem with going all-out to get that vital goal is that your team will leave gaps at the back and you may find yourself even further behind.

of the goalkeeper. There's always the possibility that, vision blocked by his own defenders, a keeper won't respond to an otherwise stoppable shot.

And when one of the midfielders moves up, there are *five* attackers well-spaced around, and in front of the goal.

The resurgence of the 4-4-2 and the decline of wings

HAVING just pooh-poohed the 4-4-2, let's take another look at it, because it represents a new trend.

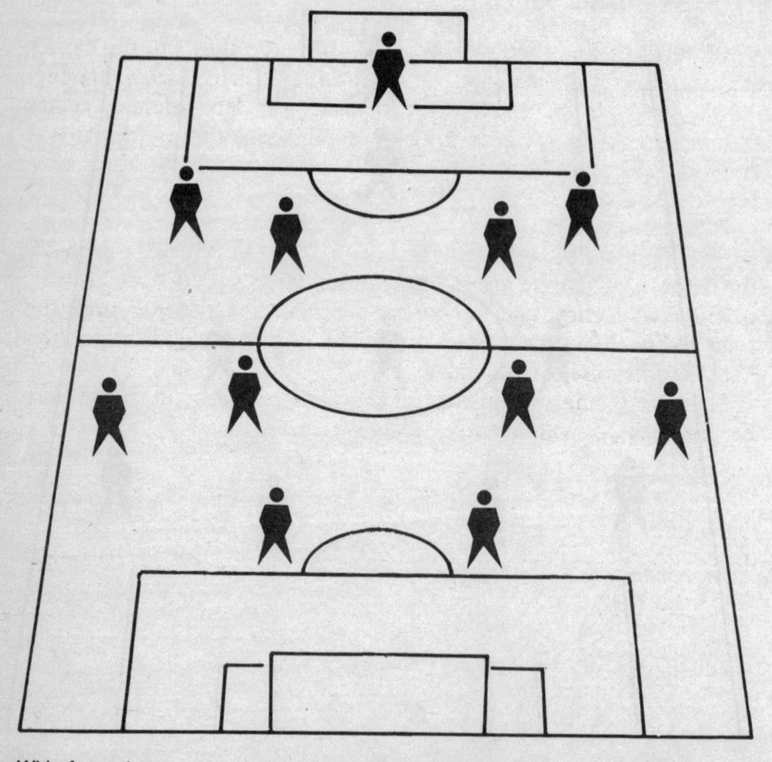

Wide front players were phased out in the 4-4-2 formation. Only two forwards were left to force their way down the middle, while the midfield became overcrowded and players had much less time before opponents were snapping at their heels.

Probably without realizing it, Sir Alfred called attention to what many coaches are beginning to believe — *that in world-class soccer the wings are dinosaurs.* (To give the 4-2-4 its due, similar thinking applies, in that the left wing spends more time as left-half.) Scoring occurs from in front of the goal, and balls crossed into that area from the side are too easily cleared away by today's larger and stronger fullbacks. The current belief is that it's better to have more full-timers in the middle, and leave the outsides to enterprising part-timers.

Who's playing where?

THE more a team plays together, and the better they get, the harder it is to tell at a glance what formation they're supposedly playing. You'll see right halfbacks over towards the left sideline, center halfbacks angling towards the corner, fullbacks taking part in the offense, and wings harassing a ball carrier back near their own team's penalty area.

Oftentimes, it's a unison move by several players. For instance, when a right fullback gets control of the ball, and carries it upfield, the defense will rotate around behind him. The sweeper moves over to fill his vacancy, the left-fullback becomes a sweeper, and the right halfback — likely to be out of the immediate action — drifts back into defense on that side.

In the final analysis, instead of "formations," a better word may be "line-ups" — who *begins* playing where.

Are We Entering The Age Of "Formationless" Soccer?

SINCE formations are anything but that, as soccer is played, and the top teams in the world are those that allow players the greatest freedom to innovate, we may see "formationless" soccer taking over. It's not as drastic a thought as it may seem, more of a natural extension of what's already happening.

Drawing from his observations of successful teams in recent World Cup competitions, Chyzowych claims that with the development of players able to play all positions with more-or-less equal ability, teams can now throw all ten field players into an attack, with confidence that they will be just as quick to respond, and as effective on defense.

"A totally trained, well-rounded soccer player has evolved who can play in all parts of the field. This total player must serve as the model for the development of the American player. The emphasis must be placed on eliminating positional players and establishing positionless players," noted Chyzowych.

Positionless play doesn't mean a return to pre-pass days, where everyone milled around with no more purpose than to pursue the ball . . .quite the opposite. It's the ultimate application of "movement off the ball," which makes the best use of individual talent, physical and mental.

For instance, in the standard 4-3-3, a midfielder in control of the ball can direct it behind the defense towards the corner, knowing the designated wing will be in position to run it down. In positionless play, the only difference is that *anyone* may make the break towards the corner, from any direction, while others are "flooding the zone," to support and exploit. Unsure who is where, you can imagine the extra pressure placed on the defense to constantly, and quickly, adjust to the unexpected.

This illustration suggests that the wingless 4-4-2 could be considered the beginning of modern positionless play. Expand the concept to all areas of the field — everyone moving to assume whatever role is appropriate — and you have the ultimate game of soccer.

If the goalkeeper is the only "specialist" in soccer, then everyone else should be equally capable of trapping, dribbling, heading, tackling, blocking, shooting, and, of course, running. *At the higher levels, they usually are, so why limit their effectiveness, by limiting their role?*

On the world scene, and we'll discuss this in the chapter on the World Cup, national culture is evident in styles of play. Chyzowych, and others, feel that formationless play offers the best hope for Americans, because it may enable a natural go-for-it outlook to overcome our lack of pure skill.

Even if all these attributes exist, will it work? Not if those "anyones" are too often no ones. Positionless play demands instinctive coordination, which is hard to achieve with just one American team drawn from all over, and having a limited amount of togetherness. The fact that the Dutch have had the most success with this free-lance style suggests, that perhaps the time has come for American teams to be drawn from regions, or for the proposed new professional league that would have an opportunity to develop instinctive coordination.

Creating The 12th Player

THERE are any number of terms to suggest the same thing, that soccer strategy and tactics are aimed at outnumbering the other team, where action is occurring — and, even more important, where it is *about* to occur — thwarting the opponent's attempts to do likewise unto you.

Avoiding "dead space" — area controlled by opposing players — and going for "live space," which is open or controlled by your own players, says about the same thing. So does "movement off the ball" into open space, with its corollary, "decoying," to lure an opponent away from the action.

Pick your term, that's why all those people are running around, seemingly without a pattern or purpose to the unknowing observer — to break loose one person, who can get the ball in the net. Like chess, players must be thinking three or four moves ahead, controlling space, and diverting attention so that a rook can break unexpectedly along the sideline, and either check-mate the king, or pressure him into the waiting arms of supporting bishops and knights.

Since soccer is a comparatively low-scoring game, just one success in the entire 90 minutes can make the difference.

I settled on the 12th player term, because it adds the psychological impact of constantly being confronted with what seems to be an extra opponent. "Where did *that* guy come from?" as though the opposing coach were in cahoots with the referee to sneak someone off the bench at critical moments.

With ethical coaches, and alert referees, the teams are equal in number, so outnumbering the other team, when and where it matters, also calls for *not* outnumbering them, when and where it *doesn't* matter. Then the 12th player is going the other way.

Being at the wrong place is most likely to happen when teams adhere, too closely, to their formation, playing strictly "positional" soccer.

You'll see inexperienced, or poorly-guided teams, whose fullbacks hang back well within their own territory when their team is on the attack, even though there's nobody to guard. They are assuring that their own offense will be outnumbered, and making things tough on themselves, by leaving all that open space for the other team to structure a response.

Yes, leave one person back there, presumably the sweeper, to guard against a fast break, but get the others into the open space, or even directly supportive of the attack.

The converse is forwards hanging just onside within the midfield line, when their own goal is threatened. One is all it takes to exploit a kick into enemy territory — two forwards can't run down the same ball — so the others should be back where things are happening.

Less apparent is a player, open where it doesn't matter, like being out of reasonable reach of a pass, or allowing himself to be blocked by an opponent, so a pass would probably be picked off, or being too close, so he can't control a pass, or even gets tangled up with his own player. (It sounds quite unAmerican, but the best way to help a friend in need may be to run away from him.)

Triangles, *Triangles,* TRIANGLES!

THE vastness of the playing arena, the interchangeability of all field players, and their freedom of movement, means that soccer is a constantly repeated series of two-on-one confrontations, involving two players working together, to advance the ball against an opponent trying to mess things up.

When the three players form a straight line with the opponent in the middle, passes seldom connect. If not intercepted, they're deflected. The partner of the player with the ball has to create a triangle, and then the passer has to do likewise, to become a passee.

The defender has to decide whether to "tackle" (to take possession of the ball or knock it away), or "shepherd" — harass without committing.

If the tackle succeeds, neat, but, if it doesn't, the tackler may take himself out of the play. (Slide tackles look great, but "stay on your feet" makes more sense.) If he shepherds successfully, he may be able to intercept the pass, or cause it to go awry. However, allowing his opponent too much space makes it easier for that person to connect with his pass, if not to his original partner, then to another moving into position.

The player with the ball, and being challenged, has his own rapid-fire decision to make: (a) try to dribble past the opponent? (b) direct a "square" pass to someone moving into a parallel position? (c) loft the ball across the field to launch a "weak side" attack? (d) set up a "give and go" — you understand what that is — or "wall pass," whereby, as the phrase implies, the partner receives a short pass and deflects a quick "first-touch" pass back to him beyond the opponent? (e) "drop pass" to someone moving up from behind? (f) "screen" the ball — keep his own body between the opponent and the ball — and look for a safety pass back to someone who can then send the ball in a new direction? That's a lot of decision-making, and very little time to weigh options. Obviously, the guy needs some help.

Talk, *Talk,* TALK!

COMMUNICATION plays a more important role in soccer than in any other team sport for one simple reason — *the ball is usually on the ground.* Players are taught to keep their heads *up* as much as possible when moving the ball — "You know it's down there, Pete. It isn't gonna run off and hide!" — but even the most skilled dribbler can't be cranking his head around looking, and he certainly can't see what's going on behind him. If he's being closely marked, he has to focus on that threat, and has even less opportunity for sight-seeing.

Coaches are constantly reminding players to "talk out there!" to let the person with the ball know where they are, and "keep it simple!" which means don't talk too much. There isn't time for lengthy discussions. (Also, *don't* talk when you haven't anything worthwhile to say, like yammering for the ball when there's no way the guy can get it there.)

For a moment, put yourself out there on the field. A loud and clear *square* is all it takes to let him know you're coming up from out of his vision into a lateral position not too far away. He doesn't even have to see you to make a relatively safe pass. The same signal from too far away is useless, and even hazardous, since a lengthy lateral pass invites interception, and a break-away opportunity for the other team.

Back lets him know that you have moved into position five or so yards behind. Again, a relatively safe outlet for a quick heel pass, but useless if you're too close — a heel pass is at best approximate — or an opponent is within intercepting range.

Taking possession of the ball, especially when it's in the air, requires a player's full attention, so it's up to someone nearby to help him decide what to do with it. *Man on* — an opponent is right there, so he has to do something quickly. *Turn* — an opponent is coming up, but he has just enough time to shift direction, and avoid the charge. *Time* — there's no immediate threat, so he can "settle" the ball, and then decide what to do.

Actually, the most productive form of communication isn't vocal at all, it's movement easily spotted by the player with the ball. Then, maybe a hand signal that the defender can't see, indicating an opportunity for a give-and-go, or wall pass.

To describe all examples of position-changing tactics would tax our readability limit, but there are a few that are fundamental, and easy to evaluate from your viewpoint.

"Overlapping" side-line runs

WITH action in the middle or other side, players can race up along the sideline from midfield, or even defense, to create a numerical advantage for an attack. It's fundamental to formationless play, and illustrates how the 4-4-2 creates wings where none exist.

In the more prevalent 4-3-3 it most frequently involves a wing forward and a wing halfback. Typically, the forward has come back into midfield to receive a pass, and then, rather than zapping outside along the sideline as expected, breaks inside towards the goal. As the defender reacts to intercept, the halfback overlaps towards the area usually occupied by the wing (and now deserted by the defender) to become an extra forward.

Seeing the halfback dashing past, the defender is caught between staying with his man, or retreating to cover his area. Man-to-man prevailing — and the rule being always to mark the man with the ball — other defenders have to adjust quickly.

If the ball does go to the overlapper breaking towards the corner,

The player on the flank has made an overlapping run, coming on to the ball pushed forward by an opponent who has eliminated two defenders.

the sweeper usually angles across to prevent him from moving into shooting position. If one or more midfielders don't drop back quickly, the defense is outnumbered.

What is the wing fullback on the attacking team doing while all this is happening? He's moving up to replace his halfback. It's pretty safe as long as the attack is in progress, and others are ready to cover for him should things go wrong.

Nor is there any reason why the fullback can't continue all the way into the penalty area where he becomes a total nuisance, since nobody is assigned to pick him up. *He becomes the 13th player at that point.*

Rotating in offense and defense

Rotary movement . . .embodying lateral and angular running . . .is intrinsic to soccer because of the space, and, therefore, the time involved. The field, you'll recall, is almost as wide as it is long, and there are no limits on player movement.

Like an overlapping run from behind, extra pressure can be placed on the defense by someone in the middle "looping" or "swirling" around towards the corner. You can envision how it would be done with the 4-4-2 where there's that extra midfielder available for opportunities with minimal risk.

Rotating on defense is really more a matter of preventing the other team from exploiting their 12th player, brought about by overlapping, swirling, or looping . . .or by individual effort.

For example, if an attacker with the ball eludes the wing fullback, someone . . .usually the sweeper . . .has to come across and pick him up. Otherwise he has an open pathway to the goal. Of course that leaves a dangerous hole that must be plugged quickly, which leaves another dangerous hole that must be plugged quickly. And so it goes, with defenders rotating, and midfielders, and even forwards coming back to help out.

Setting up "outlet" passes

THE (acting) wing chases the ball towards the corner hoping to swerve into shooting position, or bend it across in front of the goal. What he finds is that the endline curtails forward motion, the sideline curtails sideways, and that ugly fullback blocks his motion (and kicking foot) towards the goal.

That's when he needs a friendly face moving up to accept an outlet pass. With defense attention focused on the threat he poses, and on other attackers moving into striking position, the wing *midfielder*, is open. Likely to have some time, he can direct the ball back to the wing breaking towards the goal, or shift the attack to the weak side, lofting a pass for the other wing.

Or, if he wants to make a real nuisance of himself, he can carry the ball ahead, and force a defender to come out and pick him up. (He shouldn't be able to do that, of course, since an opposing midfielder should be on his case, but — mistakes, *mistakes,* MISTAKES.)

"Flooding the zone"

A MORE soccer like term might be "overloading," but it's the same concept — *creating a numerical imbalance in one area to exploit a weakness.*

I use a football like term here, because the tactic is most apparent on the gridiron. A rookie cornerback or free safety with a gimpy knee gets extra attention from the opposing quarterback in obvious ways. An outside halfback or fullback, not quite up to his mates in talent, speed, or experience, may draw similar attention, but it may be less obvious to an observer.

To begin with, until half-time the coach can't gather everyone together and pass the good news. The players have to pick up on the opportunity themselves. With no set plays to exploit the weak link (of course pun intended), the team can only shift their offense surreptitiously, and hope the other guys don't notice too soon.

"Shift their offense" may not mean what one would assume. Since the vulnerability will probably be an outside position, flooding to break through or around at that angle and distance, is no direct threat to the goal, and surely sounds the alert. What they really want to do is focus more action in that area, and draw other defenders over to back this guy up, which leaves space for flooding or overloading in the middle or far side. It's called playing the "weak side" — *launching the attack where the ball isn't, but will be if all goes well.*

Crossing passes for weak side attacks

BECAUSE the ball travels through the air faster than humans can move along the ground, soccer offers opportunities for what may be termed "reverse" flooding or overloading. You develop a play along one side of the field, drawing attention that way, and you suddenly loft the ball across the field to a wing halfback or forward that nobody's paying attention to.

Granted, it may be a low-percentage play, but it's also a low-risk play. Usually the worst that can happen is that the ball goes out of bounds in the other team's territory. If it does connect, that player has plenty of space to work with, and others have time to move inside the penalty area for a return pass.

Minimizing a striker

WHEN the other team has a scoring threat able to outrun or outmaneuver his assigned fullback, the defensive equivalent of flooding or overweighting is keeping the ball as far away from that guy as possible. He's probably the center-forward, so you try to move the ball along the outside. You'd have a numerical imbalance towards whichever side that might be so as to keep someone between the ball and the striker.

Chances are, as time goes by, our menacing striker will begin ranging far and especially wide to get into the play, become less of a frontal threat, and his teammates will make low-percentage passes trying to get the ball to him.

(Closing Thought)

Something you may now be wondering, I saved for last. What about the reverse two-on-one . . .*two people converging on the player with the ball?* It generally doesn't produce desired results for a couple of reasons. First, two players converging fast are likely to obstruct each other. A quick flip past or outside them, and the dribbler is off to the races. Second, for another player to attack he has to leave his man unguarded. That's why man-to-man marking and pursuit is the first order of business, and zone — someone else challenging — is only as necessary.

The Full-Court Press

THE theory that when your team has the ball everyone plays offense doesn't seem difficult to grasp and apply. It's reinforced every time your goalkeeper has the ball and holds it until his players are ready to do something with it. A brief-enough pause but sufficient to get people thinking offense.

The flip side, of course, is that when the other team has the ball, everyone plays defense. Not that there's anything earth-shaking about the concept — it applies just as much when a football, basketball or puck is intercepted — only that some players have to be reminded, especially forwards.

Again, it's a matter of space, and its effect on reactions. On a rink or court, anyone intercepted can quickly get back in the action. A soccer forward, who may have sprinted 30 yards only to have the ball stolen away, has to force himself to reverse his momentum and challenge the thief.

"Why bother? — I'll never catch him." With his own goal only vaguely visible in the distance, and out of breath besides, it's a natural thought process to let someone else challenge, forgetting that whoever does, has to leave an opponent unguarded in the midfield.

Actually, a forward often can overtake the fullback, since one can't move at full speed and still control the ball. Sensing a challenge coming up from behind, the fullback has to get rid of the ball before he's an effective cog in the counter-attack.

The defensive responsibility of the forward begins when the other keeper has the ball. As the first element in his team's offense, rather than punt the ball, and chance it being driven back in his teeth, the keeper would prefer to throw it to a wing fullback on the weak side, away from where the shot came from, before the other team can react and shift.

It's up to the forward on that side to full-court press — to move into position to intercept the ball, or at least discourage the maneuver. If he's late getting there, then he has to harass the fullback, and block him from moving upfield. (If he's going to get beaten, it should be to the outside rather than the inside, another soccer truism that applies everywhere.)

Where the full-court press should *not* apply is harassing the keeper when he has the ball. You'll see forwards fronting the keeper, trying to interfere with the release . . .dumb play!

First, because if he does interfere, he'll be charged with obstruction. Second, it's not likely the keeper will obligingly kick the ball in the forward's stomach, or throw it in his face, although he might like to. And, third, because while he's standing there everyone else is moving away, so if the ball is snared by someone on his own team, he's blatantly offside.

What he should do is shadow the nearest field opponent, so the keeper can't get it to him. At least then he can easily get back onside during the passage of the ball.

The Importance of Team Style

I DON'T mean how players dress, who they consort with, or whether they are photographed in the proper night spots. By "style" I mean what kind of game they play, whether primarily positional or free-wheeling, defensive or offensive, controlled short-ball or scrambling long-ball, etc.

What makes style a predominant factor in soccer is that it takes so long to develop, to bring about the intuitive coordination among all players in all that space, and that it cannot be changed very much from one game to the next. Shuffling a few players around may enhance the team's performance, but only within the framework of their style of play. You can't convert a controlled short-ball team to a scrambling long-ball team, or the other way around, overnight . . .not over a week or over a month.

The best policy is for a team to concentrate on playing its "own game" to the best of its ability. The team that can impress its style on the other, even if it's a theoretically inferior style, has the advantage.

There are all kinds of parallels we're familiar with. The full-court press in basketball, or aggressive forechecking in hockey, can throw off a better team's timing and force turnovers. An all-out blitz hurries a dangerous quarterback into releasing too soon. You can see it in tennis, where a defensive specialist can drive a supposedly better player up the wall by returning everything he hits.

What's liable to happen is that a better team (or individual), out of annoyance and/or frustration, will abandon their game plan, and play "down" to the other team's level – and into their waiting hands.

Falling into the Kick-And-Run Trap

THE easiest thing to do with a soccer ball is kick it. Even I can do that. There are those teams whose fullbacks and midfielders delight in booming the ball heavenwards, frightening birds, veering aircraft, drawing rain, and provoking ooooh's and aaaah's from spectators. It's annoying and lousy soccer, but Kick-And-Run can win out over a more skilled team.

For one thing, there's always the threat of a breakaway goal. The "Run" part of Kick-And-Run suggests a speedy forward hanging around the sweeper in the center of the field, and maybe another poised to chase the ball down along a sideline. This threat forces the defense to hang back, rather than support an attack in their usual style.

Seeing balls sailing over the heads of the defense also creates problems, if not panic, for the goalkeeper. If an attacker has a step on a pursuer, he may have to abandon the goal to intercept; a tad too soon or too late, and the attacker then has a shot at an unprotected net. Timing a ball descending from the heavens is tricky, and, if not caught, can bounce over the keeper's reach for a cheapie goal.

In the spirit of things, Kick-And-Run midfielders like to take long shots on goal. A low-percentage tactic, but one can sneak under the crossbar or beside the upright, or deflect onto the foot of an onrushing forward.

Even if none of the above occurs, the Kick-And-Run style of play forces the other team to constantly race back and regroup, which becomes exhausting as well as frustrating. Midfielders get cricks in their necks watching the ball sailing on high. Forwards don't have time to support their midfield and defense. "There it goes again!" — it gets tough on the molars.

Without being aware they're doing it, the better team finds themselves playing the same kind of long-ball game. I suppose it's an unconscious taste-of-your-own-medicine response, but, since the Kick-And-Run's are used to that style of play, chances are they can do it better.

Well, if Kick-And-Run is such "lousy" soccer, how come it seems to work so well? It doesn't, if the more skilled team can get back their own control game, and exploit the underlying weakness of long-ball kickers — that they like to move *up* on the ball. Make them run sideways, or especially turn and run back, and they can't drive the ball downfield.

Use short, angled passes to set things up, and give them little to pound. Attacks along the outside, or into the corner, or just over their heads, force them to match skills which should, eventually, swing the advantage back where it belongs.

There's another drawback to power kicking that can be exploited, albeit with some risk to life and limb. The harder a ball is kicked, the further it will rebound off a block. Rather than flinch (certainly understandably!), forwards and midfielders running right into a kick, may get a rebound that serves as a through pass beyond the defense. If they just keep going, they may have what amounts to a breakaway.

Defeating the Stacked Defense

DURING the 1950's when the *catennacio* virus was rampant, and again in the 1970's, the style was to play very conservatively with emphasis on defense, and only occasionally attacking. While spectator pressure forced more emphasis on scoring, there still are times, especially when protecting a lead or just playing for a tie, that a team will replace a forward with an extra fullback, and throw up a throng in their penalty area.

In discussing formations, I mentioned one possible solution — switching in kind. If a team adds an extra fullback, you add an extra forward to convert a 4-3-3 to a 3-3-4. That restores the balance, and adds more depth to your attack, but doesn't give you the 12th player you want.

Patience is now in style. To plunge ahead, and try to penetrate directly, is to invite the defense to kick the ball away — into your territory or over the sideline — to eat up time. A better idea is to spread the defense — move the ball around as in basketball, just beyond reach, so they have to move out or sideways, while your forwards are zigzagging around seeking a brief opening which, from that close, the midfielder can reach with a pass (preferably lofted so that the defense can't kick it away).

One ploy, for instance, may be for the center-forward to suddenly dash towards one corner. Seeing him approaching, the wing then crisscrosses into the center. This creates momentary confusion among the defense as to who is responsible for who. (Even if an aerial ball towards the center-forward/wing goes over the sideline, it's only a throw-in for the other team. It may go off a defender, over the endline, for a corner-kick.)

Or, a forward can abruptly sprint out of the penalty area for a short (and safe) pass from the midfielder, who then sprints ahead for a return pass. Again, a momentary delay, and spreading in coverage, which may leave just enough of an opening.

Another reason for frequent short thrusts, rather than long shots, is the possibility, with bodies hurtling about, of causing a defensive foul near the goal, and an ensuing penalty-kick. (At this point, who cares *how* they score as long as they do!)

Dealing with a Physical Team

I DON'T know why I bring this one up, because there's no pat solution to a team that is constantly flirting with charging, obstructing, dangerous play, and unsportsmanlike conduct infractions. As long as the referee allows them to do so, they'll keep it up.

To retaliate is a mistake, because it's just what the ruffians want. Referees may miss the foul, but they'll always catch and penalize the retaliation. (I don't know why, they just do.) Besides, stooping to their style means abandoning your style.

Chances are, the reason they're physical is to disguise lack of talent. To swing things the other way, the beleaguered team should use a lot of movement and quick short passes. If the ball is gone when a collision takes place, it's an obvious foul. Even if the pass doesn't connect, the offended team has a direct free-kick, which will eventually take its toll.

Here's where we may learn from our role-models abroad. Ever notice, in their televised games, how a guy suddenly, and often for no visible reason, flops on the ground and writhes around clutching his ankle in agony, and keeps doing so until the referee notices? It doesn't always result in a foul, but it alerts the referee to keep an eye on the other guys.

Flopping and writhing are techniques we would do well to learn. *Forget John Wayne, remember John McEnroe!* The "innocent victim" of foul play (or bad officiating) usually gets a break later.

Having A Ball With Restarts

BY definition, a "set-play" in any sport is when action resumes after a stoppage. They're all set-plays in football, however, in soccer, it's only when the referee signals that the ball is out of bounds, or if he calls a foul, which (to remake a point) is entirely his decision. And, because there is no line of scrimmage or positional restrictions, other than the ten-yard and offside rules, a more appropriate term is "restart."

Have you spotted an omission — kick-offs at the start of each half, or after a goal has been scored? Since, for a change, there *are* positional restrictions, there isn't much opportunity for a set-play, as defined by players moving simultaneously according to pre-arranged plans and signals.

Now, having said that, I have to admit I once observed a goal scored by Johann Cruyff off a kick-off. Taking the pass — that makes it a direct free-kick — Cruyff suddenly booted the ball some 60 yards over the keeper's head and into the goal. What had happened was that the keeper, who had hardly expected a shot to be taken from that extreme range, had wandered out from the goal looking for four-leaf clovers, and couldn't get back in time. (Isn't that the ultimate embarrassment, though? It must have been fun explaining it to the coach.)

Was that a set-play? In a way, yes, in that probably Cruyff had noted the keeper's tendency to meander, and planned the shot. No, in that his own team was probably as startled as the opponents', and couldn't have gotten involved anyway.

Incidentally, you'll hear that between 40% and 80%, depending on who you're listening to, of all goals result from restarts. That's so much hooey! Guesswork to begin with — people don't keep statistics in soccer — and it includes penalty-kicks which skews the figures. (We'll consider penalty-kicks separately.)

Restarts tempt one to tomfoolery, but since they do work

sometimes, here we go, looking at set-play opportunities off *throw-ins, indirect free-kicks from minor fouls, direct free-kicks from major fouls, and corner-kicks.* As you can imagine, how a team uses them depends on where they are located.

Throw-ins – more than they seem to be!

THERE'S that funny hands-behind-the-head-and-arms-fully-extended-to-propel-the-ball-without-any-spin-or-twisting-of-the-body deal again. I mean, who can take a throw-in seriously? Besides, what's it doing in a game that goes to great lengths to make people forget they have upperbody appendages?

"Soccerists" people take throw-ins very seriously, because of a few other peculiarities. There are no offsides on throw-ins (I assume by now you're echoing "of course not!"). The ball is propelled from on high, so it's hard to intercept. It's more accurate, and easier to control, than a kick. And, despite the contortionist specifications, some players can throw the darn thing a mile.

So, as the thrower gets ready, there's a Chinese fire drill going on, friendlies and unfriendlies swirling around trying to influence his decision.

Within the other team's territory, the favorite is an arcing throw ahead of a player breaking past the defense along the sideline. Usually the wing, but often (as in the diagram) he's a midfielder on an "overlapping" run, while the wing cuts towards the middle. Can you see why it's a no lose tactic?

Out in the open he can create all kinds of havoc. With the sideline there, he only needs to worry about pursuit from behind, and coming over. From those angles, anyone getting to the ball first may only be able to kick it back out of bounds, which sets up another throw-in that is much closer to their goal.

The middle is a populated area, so throwing it there is chancy, unless someone is wide open. Another possibility is to heave it at someone directly in front of him, who then heads or passes it back. That's also chancy, because it's easy to foresee, and, therefore, easy to intercept on its return.

Conventional wisdom says never to throw the ball back. Once again, coming into soccer without preconceived notions, I say do it if alert coverage by the opposition leaves no better alternative.

The player back there — probably a wing fullback — is apart from traffic, and can launch an offensive into a different sector.

I do grovel to convention, though, by recommending not throwing back to the goalkeeper, even when he's easily within range. Too much can go wrong, like the ball going over his reach with the inevitable consequences.

Speaking of "throwing the darn thing a mile," I was first exposed to the most dangerous kind of throw-in during a women's game years back.

The other team had the ball on what amounted to our 30-yard line. Instead of the usual nearby maneuvering, their players clustered towards the weak side of the field, a couple breaking for the goal. How strange, I thought, but I soon learned why. With little apparent effort, a player heaved the ball about 40 yards right onto the head of the wing at the far post. An easy goal beyond the reach of our keeper — and they combined to do it again later!

Female or male, it takes just the right technique to get that kind of distance, but think of the possibilities, especially for Americans with more natural throwing potential. Maybe this is the way we can finally achieve parity with the rest of the soccer world!

The fact is, some players are fooling around with a "flip" throw — taking a running start, grounding the ball in front of them, doing a forward flip, and using the added momentum to get further distance. It's quite a sight to see, but it's nothing to try when the ball's wet.

Setting up the "second touch" on indirects

WHEN the restart occurs in one's own end of the field, there's not much point in anything elaborate. Most often a team will use the opportunity to progress the ball into enemy territory, perhaps along the line where it's less likely to be immediately intercepted, or move the ball to someone nearby, so they can carry it, or, if nothing looks promising up front, push the ball back to the keeper, and let him create his own restart towards the other side of the field.

When within scoring range, though, the idea will be to enable the second touch to be a direct shot on goal. Since the defenders (in the wall, if it's that close) can't be within 10 yards of the ball until it's touched, there's a brief window of opportunity.

The simplest play is for one person to nudge the ball sideways, or, better yet, back onto the foot of the onrushing shooter. It's also a *narrow* window, in that a low shot will be deflected, and a high shot will likely sail over the crossbar, but the chance is often worth taking.

The best way to improve chances is to set up the second touch beyond the defenders, to take advantage of the space left as they charge to block the expected shot. This requires precise timing to make sure the shooter will still be onside when the ball is touched the first time, and just enough (but not too much) chicanery to gain the element of surprise.

For example, the second-toucher may fake a power shot, and, instead, punch the ball through, or chip it over to a third participant making his neatly-timed break. If the defense buys the fake, they're going one way, while the ball and striker are going the other way. (It helps greatly if the defense is dumb enough to focus on the second-touch threat, and forget about a possible "third-touch" threat. Unlikely, but, with a good acting job, who knows?)

With so few of those opportunities, it's easy to understand why teams sometimes go haywire, and try the near-impossible (and often hilarious).

The taker of this free-kick could have tried a shot, but he has passed to a colleague who is at a better angle to the goal. Chances are, too, that the defensive wall will now break into disarray.

Take the same situation we just described with the power shooter charging, only this time, he *steps* on the ball, and keeps going. In theory, the defense anticipates a shot, and either moves up, or, if in a wall, remains frozen in place. Now the original first-toucher becomes the second-toucher, punching or lofting the ball to his partner, who just galloped into open ground in front of the terrified keeper.

It's great fun to watch, but I don't recall seeing it work. The ball is round, after all, and not nailed down. Even if he doesn't lose his balance, and sprawl headlong, he's liable to dislodge the ball, and throw his partner's timing off. (Face-down pancaking might allow a scoring shot while everyone's doubled up laughing, but I doubt that's the objective. I've never found anyone willing to practice it.)

A direct is a *direct* – why fuss with it?

AND, indeed, most teams don't try funny stuff when they have a direct that can produce a goal with a good kick. But, ironically, when the ball is *too* close to the goal, the defensive wall becomes more intrusive. With less chance of getting a shot *over* their heads, yet *under* the crossbar (and away from the keeper), some way must be found to get the ball *around* the obstruction.

The path of least resistance is to curve or bend the ball, so it slips just within an upright. Facing a skilled inswinger/outswinger, the wall will shift to block it. With no reasonable shot, it may be time for a set-play.

Just prior to the kick, you may notice the wall looking like musical chairs. A forward is trying to jostle his way in, and the defenders are trying to elbow him out. The idea is that the interloper becomes the target, and, by ducking or jumping aside, creates a gap for the shot where the keeper least expects it. (Assuming the defense lets it happen, what do you figure the odds are of the kick going through that single cavity?)

A better ploy is to pull another fake. Winding up to fire on goal, the kicker pulls back, and angles the ball to someone moving where he can get off a solid shot around the wall . . .(or, just blasts it, and hopes one of the defenders gets a sudden attack of self-preservation).

Corner-Kicks offer real set-play options

ALL other restarts — again excluding penalty-kicks for now — are random things. No two happen at exactly the same place, under the same circumstances. Corner-kicks are the exception. Different plays can be written into the game plan, and pulled out with a simple hand signal by the kicker.

Let's assume it's just how many fingers he holds up, and see what he might set in motion, assuming the ideal occurs.

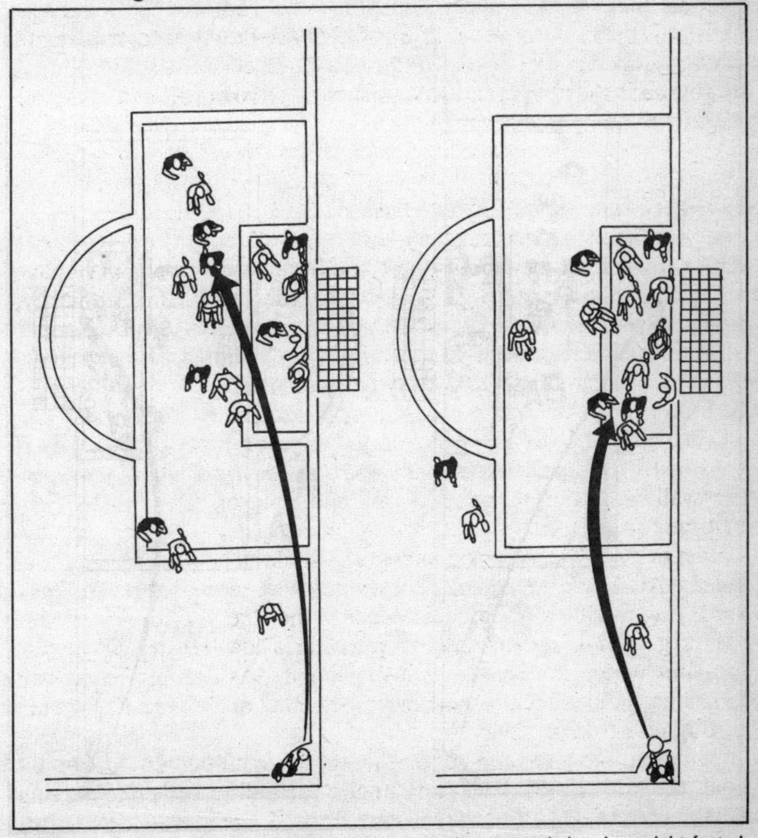

Bird's-eye view of the corner-kick. Left: An outswinging corner (taken by a right-footed player) is moving away from the goal and is ideal for the attacker who is making a run towards it. Right: Inswinger taken by a left-footed player. Goalkeepers can find it difficult to defend the post nearest the kicker, especially when opposing attackers are in the way.

(Forefinger) — *long cross beyond the far post.* The ball carries over the mob scene in front of the goal to a wing or midfielder angling in for a header. It's the most popular play, because it's hard to intercept, and whoever is moving in for the head has a clear view of the ball all the way.

(Two fingers) — *centering pass out in front.* The ball floats out away from the mob scene to the center-half in open ground, who aims a quick shot just below the crossbar. That's a tough shot to

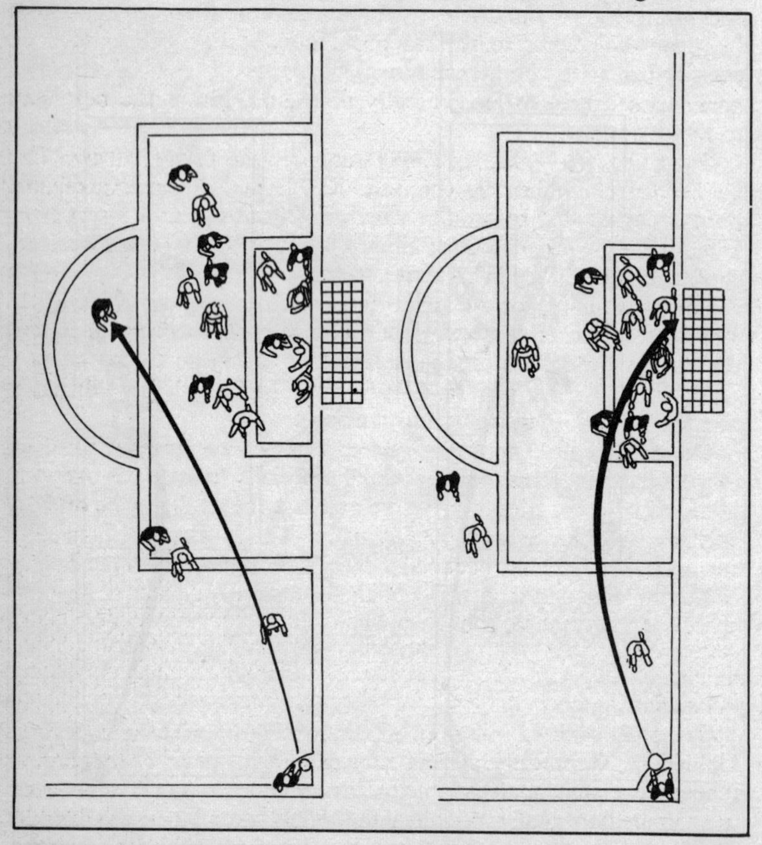

Left: The outswinger finds an attacker who is outside the penalty area and is not marked. He might try a quick shot at goal. Right: This time the inswinger is aimed at the far post and the ball might dip late in flight for a goal.

make, and may be deflected (or go too high), but it could be the best choice if the defense is jamming the goalmouth.

(Three fingers) — *a low line drive to the near post.* The ball shoots along just inside the endline for a forward to flip in before the keeper can move to it. As #1 goes beyond, and #2 goes outside the press of people, this one scoots along *behind* it all. Again, it's a matter of angles. Anyone coming back to block the ball is likely to pop it over the endline, which sets up a repeat corner-kick.

(Four fingers) — *an angled outlet pass.* The ball goes short of the mob scene to a midfielder, who has several alternatives — take his own shot, cross to the far post, move it into the middle, or even return it to the kicker moving towards the goal. The outlet pass is less likely to lead directly to a goal, but is the best way to retain control.

(Five fingers) — *an inswinger into the far upper corner.* The ball seems to be heading beyond the far post when it arcs into the far corner just below the crossbar. Because it is a direct free-kick, that's the best choice of all, but it has to be a well-nigh perfect shot, which isn't easy from about 30 yards.

That's about it for the selection, which is a good thing since we're out of fingers anyway. The main thing is to avoid dropping the ball in the middle of the defense, or too close to the keeper. And, by all means, get the ball in play. In bounds anything can happen. Out of bounds nothing can happen.

The offside rule as applied to corner-kicks always causes confusion, for players as much as spectators, and especially for officials. Anyone ahead of whoever tries to drive the ball into the goal may be offside, and it's hard to be sure in the mêlée. That's why you'll usually see attackers hanging back, and then rushing in while the ball is in the air, keeping it in front of them. But if it ricochets around, an aggressive attacker is in jeopardy.

(Closing Thought)

Generally omitted in restart discussions is the other team's goal-kick, since, technically, it isn't subject to a set-play. I'm including it because a weak goal-kick — too low or short — can be converted to an immediate goal, especially if the kick is taken by the goalkeeper. That's why you'll often see someone hovering just outside the penalty-line. Opportunities are rare, but you never know.

WANTED: Flinty-Eyed, Cold-Blooded, Panic-Proof Penalty-Kickers

THE penalty-kick is a barbaric custom more suited to the era of human-head ball. It singles out two people, who probably had nothing to do with the foul anyway, for a life-and-death confrontation with the world watching, like Clint Eastwood and Jack Palance drawing on each other in the dusty street with townsfolk peeking out from behind drawn curtains.

It may be absurd for games to be decided in this manner, but, since many are, the penalty-kick is a "restart" of special significance. Where a game is tied at the end of 90 minutes, and remains so after overtime, the outcome is usually decided by penalty-kicks — five by each team, and continuing into sudden death if necessary — so that teams have to have several practitioners of the barbaric art on hand.

Our heart goes out to the keeper who looks like he wishes he were anywhere else. (Don't think he doesn't play on those sentiments, either. He'll take any edge he can get.)

There's Palance — he's always the bad guy — just 12 yards away, able to decide when and where to fire, and Eastwood can't budge until he does. If he does move too soon, Palance gets another free shot. And, as if the odds weren't already horrendous, Eastwood remembers he left his shootin' iron on the bedside table! (I know, the analogy is sort of silly. Rather than dodge the bullet, the soccer Eastwood would have to try to catch it, but the odds are about the same. That's the point I want to make).

What chance does the keeper have? Very little, which is why our sympathies are misplaced. *The pressure is actually on the kicker.* He is expected to score at least 80% of the time. Goalkeepers can be heroes, kickers can only be goats (except to those who know better).

"If I miss this I'll never dare show my face in public!" It takes a very self-confident individual to see it as "Oh boy, what an opportunity — no way can I miss!"

Cool-headed penalty-taker has not fooled the keeper here and he is diving the correct way. But the sheer power of the kick still beat the keeper.

Penalty-kickers are born and made

A PLAYER either does, or doesn't want to be a penalty-kicker. If he doesn't, he shouldn't. He'll fail too often, and bear the scars a lifetime. If he does, he *must*, because so many others don't and shouldn't. And besides, for successful penalty shooters, running General Motors would be anticlimactic. "Penalty-kicking — it's a great place to start."

Some 192 square feet of goalmouth is a big target from 12 yards, but subtract what the keeper can cover by jumping or diving, and it's more like half that. The trouble is, the kicker doesn't know *which* half will be open. Will the keeper spring to his right or his left — or perhaps stay right where he is? (Some keepers are adept at faking a sprawl and enticing a shot that ends up right in their hands.)

Never knowing for sure, the trick is to get the ball within one of the uprights, but just barely, and with some pace. Perfection is an upper corner where no keeper can cover from his center position. Near perfection is a worm-killer within a yard of the post. With the right guess, and a mighty sprawl, the keeper may get it, but odds are against him.

Since the ball is always in the same place in relation to the goal, and the kicker has the right to adjust its placement on the spot, practice can make perfection — or near perfection. For the keeper, it's always a guessing game.

"Ignore the keeper and never change your mind!"

WHILE the kicker is making his preparations, keep an eye on the keeper. He's making his own preparations designed to delay and distract the kicker. (Keepers have to pass Indecision 101 — a course in how to drive kickers nuts without incurring the wrath of the referee.) He'll wander around supposedly getting himself together. He'll talk to the post and argue with the net. He'll retie his boot, and adjust his clothing. And, he'll take forever to settle into his position. (It takes a hard-hearted referee to intervene, as the keeper knows full well.)

What he's trying to do is get the kicker to change his mind, to abandon what he has practiced. As he prepares to shoot, thinking,

"Oh no, he knows I'm going to the right so I better go to the left," one of two things may happen. Either he misses outside the left post, or he bisects the angle, and lands the ball right in the hands of the smirking keeper.

Penalty-kickers should learn from field goal kickers. The defending team calls a time out to disrupt the kicker's concentration, but the savvy sidewinders pay no attention. They line things up, keep their eye on the ball, and do what they planned to do in the first place.

It's even easier for a penalty-kicker, since the ball is always at the same spot, and there's no snap and ball placement to worry about. The ball won't move, the goal won't move, and where Mr. Obnoxious moves shouldn't matter.

Penalty-kickers have this recurring nightmare, where, after they've gotten everything lined up, they notice the keeper with an evil grin on his face standing right where they were intending to drill the ball. If that ever happens, it's time to leave penalty-kicks to others. Your secret is out, fellah!

Are We And Professional Soccer Finally Ready For Each Other?

"READY" is the operative word, and I chose it carefully to get across a dual connotation — that Americans and soccer have to find a common ground that has thus far eluded us. The word did *not* apply to the not-so-late-and-widely-unlamented North American Soccer League. The failure of the NASL is what nay-sayers gleefully point to as proof that Americans will never support professional soccer.

However, if they didn't ignore the reality that the NASL drew big crowds for a few years or so, it would place the past and the future in better perspective, and might help in understanding what went wrong. From my own perspective as a marketing consultant, the NASL was a classic case of management failure to understand what it takes for any "new" product to succeed in a competitive market place. And, no market place is more competitive in this country than spectator sports.

People have to understand what the product is, and how to "use" it. We avoid anything that requires a complicated learning process unless, like a PC, we can't live without it. The NASL was trying to sell a product that the market, except for those thoroughly familiar with soccer, and youth, didn't understand and couldn't relate to.

The timing must be right, meaning that people must be ready to buy it when it's offered. Being too soon is worse than being too late. You know the saying — pioneers get shot, settlers prosper . . .or this one — the best mousetrap won't sell unless enough people have mice problems.

Probably seeing a similarity with Little League of earlier times, NASL magnates thought their timing was perfect, coinciding with the popularity of soccer among our youth. It proved to be a critical error in that they were much too soon for the real market — *American adults who support professional sports.*

Under pressure, Mom and Dad might take Dick or Jane to one game but that's about it. Unable to appreciate soccer, once they had done their parental duty, they would revert back to other sports, of which we have plenty.

The NASL was also much too soon to assimilate budding American stars. They weren't available yet. So, to meet the League requirements of having at least two Americans on the roster, many teams would hire naturalized foreign players.

If the NFL goes international, they may encounter the same problems. A burst of enthusiasm followed by declining interest, unless those countries can produce their own football stars.

And the new product must be sufficiently better than what's already available, to bring about a change in people's established buying habits. And it isn't whether it *is* better, but whether people *think* it is!

Even if their get-the-kids-and-they'll-bring-the-adults concept made sense, it didn't work, because the NASL failed to offer what the kids themselves perceived as a "more desirable" product.

Soccer has had to compete with *itself*

IRONICALLY, the biggest problem confronting spectator soccer has been *participant* soccer. Being a time-intensive activity, and often on a year-round basis, young players became "soccered-out" (a delightfully apt expression from my son, Philip). Rather than clamor to be taken to a pro game, they preferred other spare-time activities, which was just fine with Dad.

Like the United States Football League a few years later, one owner got impatient, and spent a good deal of money trying to beguile adults with recycled famous-name players. Other owners felt no choice, but to follow suit . . .too much, too soon, too costly. Casual spectators tired of the novelty, and knowledgeable spectators became bored. It's fun to see a Beckenbauer, Cruyff, Pelé, or Chinaglia before they retire, but not as a steady diet.

The quality-of-product drawback was stated clearly, one day, by a member of Philip's team during an NASL game.

"You know, Mr. Cook, we play almost as well as those guys." No you don't, Steve, but that doesn't matter. What matters is perception — *the very market the NASL depended on wasn't sold on the quality of the product.* There just wasn't enough good stuff going on out there to warrant making the effort to attend.

Will the MISL go the way of the NASL?

THERE must have been bystanders during NASL funeral services nodding in unison — "Ah yes, just as we always said, the NASL failed because it didn't give us bang-bang action and scoring."

What's the answer? Hockey-like indoor soccer, that's what, with the ball ricocheting off the boards, players ricocheting off each other, and double-digit scores.

Yet, one day we read that attendance at Major Indoor Soccer League games had doubled in five years, and the next day we read that several franchises were about to fold . . .NASL *déjà vu?*

Apparently, blending soccer with hockey *isn't* the answer. Like the NASL itself, bang-bang soccer aroused curiosity, and attracted spectators for a while, but after a few years the novelty wore thin.

The fundamental problem is that MISL soccer isn't soccer as such. (Isn't that what has hurt indoor football after a brief flurry of interest?)

At last, a professional structure that seems to make sense!

IT'S almost as though the United States Soccer Federation had autopsied the NASL, and determined to do everything in a different way.

Start modestly and progress at a deliberate pace. If they can work out a deal with television, fine, but don't depend on it. Forget razzmatazz, recognize that soccer is, like baseball and basketball, a plain folks, grass-roots sport. Start from the bottom, and work up, rather than at the top, and go nowhere.

At least they have the right timing in terms of access to U.S. players, which were unavailable to the NASL.

Whereas the NASL relied on spectacle appeal in big money markets, the USSF plans to replicate the German Bundesliga (National League) — and American baseball — by going wherever interest lies. They are aiming at a three-tiered structure corresponding to the Majors (professional), Triple A (semi-pro), and Double A (top amateurs). The idea is to make soccer widely available for players and spectators, then let nature take its course.

Like the Bundesliga, and unlike baseball, the idea would be for teams to move up or down, depending on how well they do on the field, and in the stands. In theory, we might see a Morgantown in the Majors, and a Los Angeles in Double A, which would be good for the game in every respect.

"But Where Are The Game Stats?"

BOB Hauser — he's the German-born coach you met before — claims Americans don't enjoy watching soccer, because we have no more patience than *rabbits*. Relax — we've been called worse things, and he has a point. We do prefer sports (and politics) that give us action in small, easily digested nibbles, and certainly no rabbit I've ever known would tolerate 90 minutes without lots of scoring; however, I think Walt Kennedy hit upon the single most important problem (no, you didn't meet him; he's a tennis player). "We've been brought up with sports that we can evaluate by statistics. There aren't any statistics in soccer that mean anything and that bothers a lot of people," observed Kennedy.

I hadn't thought of this myself, and, you know, Kennedy's right on target. Unable so far to appreciate the nuances of soccer, we seek refuge in some familiar, quantitative way to fill in our qualitative gaps. And we're not finding it. Nothing like ERA, RBI, SO, BB and E . . .or M, FG, FT, O-T, A, and PF with which to measure player performance. Football gives us enough stats to tell us what everyone was doing even in the locker room.

There it is, the newspaper account of an American Soccer League game snuggled near the bottom of E-12. First, they describe the scoring — "Jones on a header off a pass from Smith at the 34.15 point of the first half" — and, since there wasn't all that much scoring, the reporter was scratching his head trying to think of what more to say.

A brief quote from the coaches gave him a second paragraph, and then what? (Comments by the goalkeeper who let in the winning goal were better omitted.) Well, there were shots on goal, saves by keepers and fouls assessed. That gave him the mandatory three paragraphs, and a warm glow for having satisfied our supposed craving for trivia.

But what IS a shot on goal in soccer? Only the "quality" shots, those with a serious intent to score, really matter. Sometimes they don't look like shots and aren't even included in the shots-on stats. The blasts from 30 yards are always included, even though they're mostly for appearance's sake.

The most important saves, where the keeper anticipates a serious threat, and positions himself perfectly, often look the easiest. Snaring or deflecting a dangerous crossing pass, or charging out and preventing a shot from being taken, also don't appear in the "saves" box score.

This reminds me of "unforced errors" in tennis, which must be the silliest stat ever devised. *Every* error is forced — it's only a matter of degree.

"The Tornado was assessed 24 penalties, while the Whirlwind only committed 15." So, how many were majors, and what happened? Did any eventually lead to goals? I'm being silly, of course, because the reporter wouldn't have the foggiest idea. And, if *he* did, would we?

One soccer statistic that really does mean something is never listed — *the respective number of corner-kicks.* If you think about it, the team deflecting more balls off defenders, and over the endline, must be dominating. Sometimes, when a game cannot be decided any other way, it's decided on that basis.

I'll probably come to regret having said this, because I can foresee what's going to happen: All the numbers fanatics will come out of hiding, gather in hand-rubbing ecstasy, and have a soccer ball.

"Why not stats on what percentage of corner-kicks went to the far post, the near post, and out in front? Then how many were controlled by the offense and the defense?"

"Good, *Good!* And if corner-kicks are important then goal-kicks must be too, in the opposite sense. Now we can talk about corner-kick/goal-kick ratios."

"Yeah, and how about keeping records of how far goal-kicks go, and what percentage are controlled by which team?"

"You know, guys, we could do the same sort of thing with throw-ins, too. Like who got how many, and what percentage were controlled by their own team."

"And don't forget the most important stat of all — how many shots a forward takes, and what percentage go in! Hey, you know I'm beginning to *like* this game!"

Most people reckon that Argentina's Maradonna is the greatest player in the world today. Would statistics prove otherwise?

(Closing Thought)

Seriously now, how are we ever going to select players for the All-Star game? Without statistics, we'll never be able to recognize excellent players on weak teams. Maybe we'll just have to accept the fact that there can be no Pro Bowl in soccer. I've often wondered why there's one in football.

And Where's The TV Coverage?

IN our world, if something isn't on the tube, it doesn't exist. Everybody knows that. USSFers claim sparse telecasts of NASL games were a primary reason for the league's collapse.

There was the lack of direct revenues, of course, but even more harmful may have been the implied lack of credibility. Certainly the virtual nonexistence of soccer on television hindered my efforts to find a publisher for this spectator book.

"Maybe some kids are playing soccer, Mr. Cook, but who's *watching* soccer?"

This may make me irate, but I can't argue with them. If it isn't on the tube where people *can* watch it, who knows how many people *would* watch it if it was? . . .the old which came first, the chicken or the egg.

In post-season play, we're deluged by football bowl games, often pitting a couple of obscure colleges with sparkling six and four records. Yet there's no coverage of two well-known colleges with perfect records playing for the legitimate national soccer championship.

Well, that's because nobody calls in and asks for it, say TV programmers. More likely it's because we know it wouldn't do any good, and that's not the real issue anyway. I doubt the wires crackle with cries for mud wrestling or rock climbing, either, but we see them on television.

Demand aside, the TV industry has a couple of problems with soccer — and I mean *valid* problems — that will have to be resolved before it's a regular offering.

Absence of instant "star quality"

A LARGE measure of our fascination with our indigenous sports may be termed the Superman Syndrome. We realize that those giants of basketball, football, and even baseball are in a world apart, and we hold them in awe. Even if we don't know who they are or represent, they have tube appeal.

Players of individual sports may be of less outlandish proportions but their skills are so evident, so far beyond what we can aspire to, that they also enjoy superperson status, and, in many cases, cult status. As the TV types are well aware, these people draw the viewers, and the advertising revenues.

Soccer players are caught in no Superman's land. They're normal-sized, they function in a group environment, they have interchangeable roles — and they're seldom seen up close. One is indistinguishable from another, unless, and until, we see them perform often enough to recognize excellence. There's little chance for instant star quality that draws throngs off, as well as, on the field — and television attention.

What I fear will happen is that American television will try to over-compensate. Just as they peer into the face of the quarterback calling signals, or the pitcher going into his delivery, and ignore everyone else, during soccer games they'll entirely concentrate upon the guy with the ball, and pay no heed to the total picture. Effecting a fast and smooth transition when the ball suddenly goes elsewhere will require practice.

No commercial breaks for 45 minutes?

PLACE yourself in the role of television management confronted by 45-minute periods of non-stop action except for unexpected (unpredictable and brief) pauses.

No problem with taped telecasts, but when covering a soccer game live, when could you air those beer, car and hemorrhoid treatment commercials?

Cramming all commercials into three segments — pre-game, half-time, and post-game — is no solution. With those delightful remote control devices, the greatest invention since you know what, we'd just zap them. Using a Budweiser-kind of ID around the picture really won't satisfy sponsors, and will annoy viewers if overdone.

Setting up for kick-offs after goals offers commercial opportunities, but mighty few of them. Other restarts, like a throw-in or free-kick, are out of the question, since action usually intensifies rather than diminishes at those times.

Trying to anticipate lulls in the action and swinging away for commercials is inviting disaster. In 1966, an American network aired the soccer World Cup Final live, in which England defeated West Germany 4-2. *They missed four of the six goals!*

So, how have they solved the problem overseas? They haven't, because, until very recently, television was government operated. Now that private, commercial channels are coming on the air, they face the same quandary.

An obvious solution would be three time outs per half. Since this would introduce an artificial factor, a better solution may be some natural compromises.

Corner kicks and goal kicks involve natural pauses that may be extended for commercials.

The ball has to be retrieved anyway . . .sometimes from the stands . . .and placed in position. Further, time is required for teams to properly position themselves before the kick is taken. A reasonable added delay before the restart may allow enough time for commercials without seriously compromising the ebb and flow of the game.

But, soccer is a worldwide sport, and it may be impossible to get universal concurrence. So . . .and you may end up resenting me for voicing the thought . . .time delays may be added to allow commercials without adding artificial pauses or missing any of the play. The televised game would last several minutes longer than the actual game, but at least it would be intact and unaltered. And, "live" spectators wouldn't have to endure all those waiting periods that drive NFL attendees batty. Let's just hope reason prevails.

John Madden, where *are* you?

EVEN if overdone, Madden's quickie diagrams, coordinated with action replays, make televised football more intelligible. It would help with basketball and hockey, too, but the action is too sudden and compressed. And, there isn't time, which is the same problem with soccer.

But maybe something could be worked out, whereby a skilled soccer commentator could diagram how a goal or shot on goal came about, or how it was prevented. Time is less crucial, and illustrating tactics would surely benefit viewers . . .especially if the cameras weren't quick enough in their panning.

By all means, add cameras *behind* the goals

PERHAPS because it's automatic in football to show the trajectory of field goal tries, in this country cameras are often added directly behind the goals, to replay action in the penalty area, which results in a shot on goal. (It's also being tried elsewhere, but not yet universally.)

Since the field is almost as wide as it is long, and the confrontation between the shooter and keeper is a dramatic element, the lateral perspective is important.

(Closing Thought)

Now, I'm delighted to contradict myself — Turner Broadcasting has invested several million dollars for rights to telecast, live where possible, the 1990 World Cup from Italy. In fact, they intend to cover at least 30 games on Turner Network Television (TNT), which means an average of one game per day throughout July. And, they will telecast other international matches in months prior to the World Cup, to whet our viewing appetite.

Since the U.S. is not likely to be a major factor, that represents pretty solid faith in the future of spectator soccer in this country. Ted Turner, though, has always been an adventuresome sort.

Televised Soccer Emphasizes Space And Time

PEOPLE who begin watching professional soccer from, say England, Germany, or Italy, notice an obvious difference from our high school, or even college soccer.

The player (fullback or midfielder) bringing the ball upfield from his own end is usually given plenty of space and time to move. Rather than challenge him immediately, as we're inclined to do at amateur levels, opponents "shepherd" or "shadow" him a couple of paces away. Of course, if he gets careless and leaves himself vulnerable, or penetrates beyond the midfield line, it's a different story.

For his part, he proceeds carefully, keeping the ball close and surveying what's happening in front. If he doesn't like what he sees, he may pass sideways or back (perhaps to his goalkeeper), and assume a supporting position.

There are several reasons for this apparent leisurely pace by both sides during the setting-up process.

• *On a full-scale field, abrupt attacks seldom work.*

Since at upper levels of play everyone has excellent ball control skills, it's too easy for the ball-carrier to evade a sudden rush, or pass off laterally or behind. Either way he becomes a "12th player" in the open.

• *The defender wants to cut off angles for forward passes, or sudden runs with the ball.*

Too close and the defender can't watch the dribbler's eyes and body movements which signal intent, nor can the defender adjust to intercept a pass, or make an effective tackle. (The wise cat lets the mouse commit itself.)

• *No threat anyway, the idea is to cause him to make a mistake.*

Few goals occur by long shots, so the best defense is to keep him away, well beyond the penalty area, and gradually increase pressure to force a mistake by attempting too much, either by himself (and losing the ball), or by a long pass that's easy to intercept . . .and likely to go astray anyway.

• *For his part, the ball-carrier wants to launch an attack with the best chance of success.*

Unless he can get off a quick pass to someone breaking loose, usually along the sidelines, rushing things favors the defense. They are facing him while most of his players have their backs to him, or can only see what he's up to via peripheral vision. If nothing looks promising up there, better to move the ball back or across the field and start over.

• *Over-committing wastes energy.*

With only two subs, unproductive, energy-sapping charges and pursuits take their toll. I oppose allowing just two, but if we were to set a limit ourselves, and give our players proper fields, we'd see a more interesting American game . . .constructive rather than destructive in nature.

TV also portrays "playing for the tie" strategies.

During our more confrontational period with the Soviets, someone explained U.S. diplomatic frustration with their seeming deviousness, and obliqueness in terms of our respective favorite social games . . .*poker here, chess there.*

Based on chance and deception, poker (like "our" sports) is a series of events, each separate from the other, and each coming to a win/lose conclusion in short order.

With everything in plain sight, chess (yes, like soccer) is a series of maneuvers which may seem unrelated to each other (until later on, that is!), and which may be designed to *avoid* an immediate win/lose conclusion.

We have a saying that a tie is like kissing your sister. That's why the NFL now plays sudden-death overtimes. *Yet soccer is often played to produce a tie, and for good reason.*

In qualifying rounds of tournaments, and the World Cup, teams jockey for position. The idea is to move into the next round on the basis of points . . .a tie is worth one point . . .and sometimes all it takes is *not* losing a particular game. In fact, a tie when playing on someone else's soccer turf before loudly-partisan crowds is tantamount to a victory.

Also, aware that other (and perhaps more crucial) games are coming up where ties aren't permitted, teams want their best players in top form. Defensive play is less risky than offensive play. Even if you have no idea ahead of time, as the game progresses you can usually identify a team that's playing for a tie, or a win with minimal risk.

They play cautiously on offense, looking for just a few high-percentage scoring opportunities, and trying to keep possession of the ball. There's more back-passing than usual with the keeper exercising a key role. If they can get a lead goal, they go into a shell the rest of the way, since the other team must now score *two* goals.

They'll move most of their field players back, blocking the usual avenues of attack, and use their offensive players to place extra pressure on approaching ball carriers. (If a team is naturally defense-oriented, they may play that way from the outset until, and unless, they fall behind.)

The danger to the team needing a victory is that, as time passes and frustration mounts, they'll over-commit, and do silly things. They may fall into the habit of releasing the ball too soon before a receiver is in position, or conversely, holding onto it too long, and running into double coverage.

Or, fed up seeing passes picked off or deflected by massed defenses, they may advance their own defenders so far up field that they become vulnerable to fast-break attacks behind them.

As we saw when discussing styles of play, since soccer is so much a game of intuitive coordination, changing from one style to another within a game is almost impossible. However, when you have to get a goal, and time is running short, you have no choice!

(Closing Thought)

What happens when *both* teams are playing for a tie? (It's infrequent, but possible, in qualifying rounds when both are in position to advance, as long as they don't lose to each other.)

Then you're watching Alphonse and Gaston en masse . . .or the early rounds of a fight where both boxers, wary of the other's punching power, are feeling each other out.

What's likely to happen is not much for a while...not until one guy gets a wide-open shot, and takes it successfully. (No striker, however polite, can resist an engraved invitation.)

Then it's Katie Bar The Door. As though slapped in the face, the other team throws caution to the wind, and it's a real fracas.

If they manage to score the equalizer, things revert to a cautious you-first-no-be-my-guest waltz.

If neither team needs to win, why play at all? . . .because they have to, and the results will affect their next meeting, which is a single-elimination, win-or-lose affair. To misquote Milton, "If not victory, then revenge."

What's Behind Violence Associated With Soccer?

JUST breathe the word "soccer" in any gathering and the subject comes up. First there's curiosity and well-what-would-you-expect smirks, and then concern whether we'll have to deal with violence ourselves as soccer gains its place here as a spectator sport.

Don't even bring it up, advocates of soccer urge me, because I could impair our professional development, and even our staging of the 1994 World Cup Finals. Besides, they claim, it's been blown all out of proportion by people who see the burgeoning popularity of soccer threatening "our" sports.

Even if I wanted to omit it, guys, I couldn't do so without losing credibility. Everyone reading this book knows there's a violence factor, so I figure the best approach is to explore the reasons, drawing largely from testimony of people, like Rippon, with all-too-personal experience.

Let's begin by clearing up a few likely misconceptions . . .and doing away with some of the smugness we may be feeling.

It seldom involves the players. A "ruffians" game it may be, but you don't see the bench-clearing brawls that are all-too-frequent in our own baseball, hockey, basketball, and even football.

One reason is that a soccer referee will "red card" a deliberate perpetrator. The "laws" — the appropriate term here — are clear about that. Since the dismissed player cannot be replaced, his team plays short the rest of the game. Players who don't learn to control themselves don't last long! (There's no "offsetting penalties" cop-out in soccer.)

It seldom involves the true fans. I add "true" to separate out the minuscule minority who come to vent their spleen rather than enjoy the game. As we've experienced with rock concerts, just a few can start a chain reaction.

Usually, the hooliganism we read about is caused by organized gangs using a soccer game as an opportunity, even as a stage, to "get back at the system" they feel evermore detached from and put-upon by.

But dismissing it all as purely economic belies the facts. Many of those arrested have been young white-collar workers in relatively well-paid jobs. As with drug abuse, the situation is complex and deep-seated.

It often has little to do with soccer. What these gangs are looking for is a field of battle. Soccer is ideal for reasons we'll get into momentarily, but, when there's no soccer, the same gangs create havoc in seaside towns, shopping areas, theatres, and anywhere else unprotected masses gather.

And not just in deference to my British publishers, but because it's a fact, what happens there happens throughout Europe. I myself encountered unpleasantness in the stands in Sweden (of all places!) during the Gothia Cup tournament ten years ago.

It's fair to say that the players and true fans are the most distraught by violence. Yet it's a self-fueling problem, since the orderly element is staying away, and the troublemaker element is growing percentagewise, if not numerically.

The reasons why violence may happen in soccer-tradition countries suggests reasons why it's unlikely to happen here. Mostly it's a matter of fortunate happenstance.

In most other countries, soccer is *it*

LOCAL, regional, and national emotions are triggered by this one team sport whereas we have several team sports that diffuse intensities.

"Okay, you got us in football, but just wait for the basketball (hockey or baseball) season!"

As those countries adopt more team sports, and the process is already underway, soccer intensities are sure to lessen.

Then there's proximity and traditions of mutual animosity

WE'RE aware that elsewhere in the world, especially where there are less expanses than over here, neighboring and nearby nations have been elbowing each other for centuries. And before nations were formed . . .relatively recently as history is measured . . .neighboring and nearby communities functioned as small-scale nations squabbling over their turf.

By way of contrast, how many walled cities were there in the United States? (Stockades don't count. They were intended to keep the Native Americans out!) And is there any significance that, from roughly the 10th through the 15th centuries, Europe was called a "feudal" society?

For example, the Derby County and Nottingham Forest clubs in England, long-time feudal rivals, are just 16 miles apart. Where cities, and for that matter, countries, are so close together, crowds inside and mobs outside the stadium are almost evenly divided between "us" and "them," which is like the proverbial ticking bomb.

Again by way of contrast, a few hundred Redskins' fans scattered among 50,000 Cowboys' fans are unlikely to start trouble.

"NO FOOTBALL COACHES ALLOWED"

ANY American first seeing one of these signs posted before ramps exiting arterial highways in England may wonder what they have against Joe Gibbs or Mike Ditka. Translated, what they mean is that busloads of riotous gangs coming to a game can bloody well keep going, or better yet, go back where they came from, and create havoc there.

They help explain another cause of the problem . . .*that the rowdies gather beforehand and come in groups.* Likely to be well-oiled (sometimes well-armed) before they arrive, they're trouble looking for a place to happen. Because our rivalries are so far apart . . .and so new . . .the "football coach" phenomenon is uncommon.

Standing room crowds almost assure problems

Largely because our stadiums are newer, standing room is very limited and spread around. We generally don't allow people in without seats, which means everyone is pretty well intermingled, and sudden mass movement is almost impossible.

In older stadiums in other countries, large numbers of spectators

A peculiar aspect of soccer in most countries is that many spectators prefer to watch standing up. Theorists claim that all-seater stadiums would prevent violence. Cynics say that the thugs would just use the seats as weapons.

stand . . .many of them, apparently, by choice . . .which generates two kinds of problems.

One is what we read about most frequently . . .large numbers of spectators being crushed or trampled, as in Sheffield in 1989 with people coming in, and in Moscow back in 1982 with people going out. Things inadvertently got out of control, and mistakes were made, with tragic consequences.

When standing room crowds are allowed, warring factions can gather. Eventual trouble is almost inevitable (and hard to contain), since the perpetrators can move around, fade from sight, and evade the stadium authorities.

Maybe the next time we grumble about how long it takes to get back to our cars we'll pause, take a deep breath, and look on the bright side. At least we'll *get* there eventually!

A little knowledge can be a dangerous thing

MOST spectators in other countries understand soccer inside and out, or think they do. Furthermore, it's all spread out there where they can see every move of every player, and every call made by the referee . . .not like football, where fans seldom have any idea why one of several officials has dropped a flag.

Soccer being a contact/non-contact sport, there's a fine line between legal and illegal collision, and many of both take place with players coming together at high speeds. Seeing one's favorite writhing on the ground holding his shin is often enough to get even non-thuggee spectators riled up. Many players seem to carry writhing to new heights in order to draw fouls (and get the hometown fans involved, as happens in the NFL?).

Between organized gangs on the outside and emotionally overwrought spectators on the inside, it's easy to understand the threat of violence. Get them together and it erupts.

(Closing Thought)

Could it be that American football appeals to other countries because it's a *contact*/contact sport? Violence is part of the game, but in a controlled and purposeful way, and by people of heroic dimensions. While soccer offers just enough violence to stimulate (yet not satiate) some people's craving, football gives them all they need. (By the way, I acquired this notion from a British professional soccer player, so don't guffaw at me!)

Getting Ready For The 1994 World Cup

OF COURSE, we'll be seeing a lot of international soccer before 1994. ESPN has been televising U.S. games in the 1990 World Cup qualifying round, and TNT will be televising at least 30 final round games from Italy, as well as exhibition games along the way. And don't be surprised if a major network grabs the chance to show the 1991 Women's World Cup in China, which is sure to include the United States. (A "first" in every way, the viewer appeal would be unprecedented!)

This being the case, let's wrap things up by taking a look at two aspects of the game at its most sophisticated levels. *How and why different nations have different styles of play - and how and why the game is changing while remaining the same.*

Because there are so many people out there with so much space and time to work with, soccer uniquely reflects — expresses may be more appropriate — the physical characteristics, social and family traditions, educational, cultural, and even political structure of a nation . . .and, to a great degree, the prevailing climate.

Yet, because soccer at the highest levels is conducted on an international stage, national teams learn from each other. Also, the fact that more nations have elevated their level of play has brought about a lessening of differences. Nevertheless, in countries where soccer is played, there will always be certain distinctive soccer characteristics peculiar to each of these countries, that will be retained.

At the time I'm writing this, my best reference source is *FIFA WORLD CUP - MEXICO '86*, the official report of the final round played that year. A beautifully constructed volume, replete with color photos and diagrams, it analyzes the 24 teams and 52 games in detail. It's obviously a work of dedication by several knowledgeable observers, and I hope I don't do them too great an injustice by my American interpretations.

Because soccer *is* a worldwide sport, structural change is hard to effect. Yet, the structure of the World Cup Finals *has* changed to reflect elevation of play throughout the world.

First, beginning with the 1982 World Cup in Spain, the number of teams invited to the élite gathering was raised from 16 to 24. Thus, South Korea, Iraq, and Canada made their World Cup final round debut in Mexico.

By the way, if you want to ace a soccer know-it-all, ask him, with proper innocence, when the U.S. *first* played in a World Cup final round. He'll likely say in 1950, which is the *last* time prior to 1990. Actually, you've got him on two counts. The U.S. appeared in the *original* finals in Uruguay in 1930, and again, in 1934, in Italy.

Why has this been overlooked? Here's where the know-it-all may trump your ace. Since the event was new, there were no qualifying rounds, and it wasn't even called the "World Cup." (The case may have to go to arbitration.)

Second, and also in 1982, to make the elimination/progression process fairer and more competitive, the Federation adopted a format we were very familiar with ourselves.

For the opening round, the teams were divided into six groups of four each, playing three games round-robin style. Prior to 1986, only the top two teams in each group moved on, which meant that a deserving team in a tough group might not survive, while a lesser crew in a weaker group could survive.

Now, the four best third-place teams, determined by win/lose/tie points, join the top 12 in the second round.

In previous World Cups, opening the door for a few third-placers wouldn't have accomplished much, since a predictable group of teams dominated. But as more nations were putting out top-quality teams, notably from the Third World, the Federation agreed that the structure should reflect the new reality of worldwide balance.

Yes, it's much like our own professional League-to-play-off system, especially paralleling the NFL, except that these 24 soccer teams were already into the "play-offs." With more than 100 nations fielding teams, they had to have survived months of "league" play to have made the final 24. (Unlike the NHL and NBA, you won't find any teams with losing records among them!)

From this point, the 16 survivors played single-elimination games, as in any tournament. In 1986, ten were European, four South

American, one a Mexican team, and a surprise in the form of "Third World" Morocco. It'll be interesting to see how the balance shapes up in 1990, as it may prove a portend for 1994, when we will automatically be entered as the host team.

Return to the Offensive

I'LL be quoting directly from the Official Report occasionally, so I better warn you that, presumably written in Spanish and translated into who knows how many tongues, some of the expressions in our tongue are delightfully and maybe unintentionally forthright.

FIFA observers noted with pleasure that "most teams tried to play a more offensive style," and that "the players took more risks, the style of play by most teams was characterized by a fast pace." If so, then how come the 132 goals scored were fourteen fewer than were scored four years earlier in Spain?

There are two apparent reasons. Because the teams were more evenly matched, there were few instances where a powerhouse could run up the scores. *A greater factor was the anticipated playing conditions.* In addition to July heat and humidity, most games were played at high altitudes. Being allowed only two subs, even the most aggressive teams had to pace themselves to avoid running out of gas late in the game.

What sometimes happened, though, is what the Report refers to as the "risks of exaggerated adaption" — (adaptation in our lingo).

Since conditions in Italy and the U.S. won't be all that great in July, either, why isn't the World Cup being held in the spring or fall? Good question. I suppose it's to allow the maximum number of spectators to make the journey, and, in many countries, all non-essential activities close down during July. (Why not in this country? Good question.)

The results of "exaggerated adaption"

THE importance of playing "your own game" implies the hazards of departing too far. In any sport, there's a fine line between just enough and too much adaptation. It's even harder to strike the right balance in soccer, because imbalances are hard to detect, and, without pauses, harder to correct.

In 1986, some teams over-emphasized economy of movement, and took themselves out of their own preferred style of play.

For instance, Italy, a perennial favorite, was eliminated by France in round 16. Accustomed to a Latin-like attacking style with three or four players likely to threaten the goal at once, preparing to play in Mexico, they shifted to short passes and limited movement. It was contrary to "the footballing tradition of Italy," and resulted in setting up too few scoring opportunities with more than one attacker.

The U.S.S.R. also was unexpectedly eliminated in round 16 by Belgium. Although Iron Curtain teams are type-cast as disciplined, methodical, plodding, unimaginative — you know the pre-*glasnost* litany — as our Olympic basketball team was to discover, the Soviets "surprised the footballing world with their perfect skill and tactical variants — their displays based on the joy to play and not primarily on factors like stamina and fighting strength."

The mistake *they* made was exploding into action to score the first goal, as they did against Belgium, and then pulling back to pace themselves. Belgium scored the equalizer, and being allowed space to operate with minimal risk, increased their offensive pressure, eventually winning 4-3 in overtime.

Given that the team that scored first almost always won, the Soviets, by allowing the Belgians back in the game — twice, actually — defeated themselves. (Since the Belgians went on to the semi-finals, one has to figure they had just a little to do with it, too.)

England, along with Northern Ireland and Scotland, didn't do as well as expected, because they were accustomed to "cold weather" soccer. Presumably to keep the blood flowing in their chilly climes, these teams feature long passes, and a lot of running, a style they were hesitant to employ in Mexico.

A drastic change in playing style to meet unusual conditions is always a great risk, the Report points out.

"Players, who from their earliest youth have been familiar with just one style of play, are confronted with difficulties when they have to adjust to a new style at short notice. Sometimes one had the impression that the players in certain situations did not know what to do — (leading to) an obvious feeling of insecurity."

The fact that some of the more experienced national teams fared poorly, suggests, that had the U.S. qualified, we might have done better than expected. With nothing to lose in the first place, and lacking "earliest youth" mind-set, we might have been able to use physicality, and the art of the unexpected (an upbeat way of saying tactical awkwardness) to throw a few scares, as did Canada.

"Zonal marking" makes off-the-ball play more important

IT was an inevitable in soccer football as in football football. There are now just too many highly-skilled ball-handlers out there who can't be guarded effectively by one person. Individual skills have improved to the point where most players can control and move the ball so well that a new style of play is developing.

As the Report quaintly puts it, "Those players who are able to control the ball without problems are not so often dispossessed of it and they need less strength to reconquer it."

So, instead of rushing in to tackle, teams tend to encircle the player with the ball, to cut off his opportunity to do anything constructive with it, either by dribbling or passing.

"Aggressive defenders who try to intimidate their opponents by an uncontrolled commitment and an exaggerated toughness are in the minority now."

The more attention paid to the ball-handler, the less attention that can be paid to covering his teammates, and the greater importance on their part of innovative movement "off the ball." *Now the door is ajar for a style of play that may be better-suited to our players.*

How come everyone out there is a midfielder?

ANOTHER result of improved individual skills, and emphasis on zone coverage, is the more even distribution of responsibilities among all positions. We are edging nearer to "positionless soccer," which is creating a certain amount of confusion.

As we noted when discussing formations, there's a growing tendency, as with the 4-4-2, to do without dedicated wings. They can accomplish more by playing in the midfield, which often involves participating in the defense. Conversely, the role of the fullbacks has expanded, particularly in making offensive slants all the way into wing areas.

"Taking into account all the qualities required for this position," the Report says, "one should designate the role of the fullback as a combination of midfield player and winger."

The result of wings playing back, and fullbacks playing up, can be a traffic jam at midfield . . .(and the chewing up of turf, to the annoyance of groundskeepers). Instead of three or four, now all ten field players may be in that general area, and designated midfielders have to assume "fast break" attacking roles like forwards, that they're not accustomed to.

A further result of overpopulation is that center midfield playmakers, who used to dominate are, "dying out." Almost by default, the key player now is the super-star designated attacker up ahead, exemplified in 1986 by Diego Maradona of Argentina, the eventual winners.

Given all this, what are our chances?

THERE'S good news, bad news and iffy news. First, of course, the bad news.

If the presence of a Maradona will characterize successful teams hereafter — and they have before, à la Pelé — we're in trouble. Not that, with our immense diversity of talents to draw from, there won't be players with potentially comparable speed, skill, and imagination. It will be more a problem of developing that potential which hasn't been possible previously, since we don't have a truly professional league. There is a significant glimmer of hope, however. In June 1989, the U.S. Under-21 team beat a team from England, containing players with English First Division experience, in a tournament in Toulon, France. It made headlines in England where it was felt to be more significant than that win over England in the 1950 World Cup. Then, the U.S. team was largely full of players from other countries. This time the team was built up of *American* youngsters.

Fully aware of this, and knowing its new amateur/semi-pro/pro structure won't be in place in time, the United States Soccer Federation is sponsoring an American team, pointing towards the 1990 World Cup in Italy. Team members and staff are being financed so they can dedicate themselves to gaining essential international experience. At that, the best we can hope for is to make it to the final 24 in Italy — it's unlikely we'll survive the opening round — and build for the future.

The good news is that the emphasis on midfield play, and reduced influence of a single playmaker, seems suited to our resources. Paraphrasing the Report, "Midfield stars have the tendency to wait for the ball. To run constantly clear (like a forward) is not always one of their strong points . . .All players must be in top physical shape and able to run clear constantly."

Traditional midfielders, almost because they do have superior individual skills, find it hard to exploit offensive opportunities. One reason may be that most came along during the 1970's, when defensive overkill was in style. For whatever reason, they'd much rather fuss around with the ball, and avoid taking risks. Too often, control was an end onto itself, rather than a means to set up scoring opportunities. It also figures that they may not be tops in speed and endurance.

How the U.S., with presumably less individual skill, may be able to exploit the midfield situation, can be drawn from the Report's view of how the Canadians functioned as follows:

"The attacking play was based on the physical and mental qualities of the Canadians — fastness, stamina, running power, and fighting spirit. They bridged the midfield as fast as possible and directly went for the opposing goal."

"The strong points of the Canadian team were to be found in defence. Well organized . . .with good mutual understanding . . .the physical qualities of the defenders proved quite useful."

"As soon as the defenders had conquered the ball, they tried to bring the forwards into action by long passes . . .(like the U.K. "cold weather" style which would be understandable). The midfield players immediately tried to run clear . . .to chase or fight for rebounds in order to launch their strikers again . . ."

Even if brought about by necessity, this aggressive fast-break style of play is natural to North Americans, and it upsets the rhythm of teams lacking our football and basketball heritage. However, the Report pinpointed the Canadians' fatal flaw, that they *"did not possess the necessary skill at high speed to score one of their many opportunities."* Meaning the nimble, and especially intuitive, forwards who are in the right place at the right time to finish the job.

That, I fear, may remain a weakness we'll have to compensate for. Without Pelé-Maradona strikers — very few come along, and less likely here than elsewhere — to keep defenses honest, they can take chances. They can move out, and interrupt our attack before it can culminate.

Our strength lies in our physicality and conditioning, which enables us to play a wide-open, gambling game, that can upset traditional styles of play, present unexpected scoring opportunities, and wear opponents down.

Will we do so and will it prevail? You can be sure the world will be watching — no doubt with mixed feelings — because we are the last potential power to arrive on the international soccer stage. It will be important to the future of the game that we *become* a power.

Glossary

THE very fact that soccer does have its roots in so many countries means considerable difference and confusion about terminology. Nor is there any way to include everything. So, if you don't like my definitions, you can make up your own. Not a bad thought at that since it's time we left our imprint . . .on terms as well as turf.

Advantage Rule — If, in the referee's opinion, whistling a foul would benefit the team whose player committed the foul, he may signal play to continue with no penalty. (Many referees suggest a hockey-like version where the penalty *is* assessed automatically when the offended team loses the ball. That way the advantage would always be properly applied.)

Back Pass — When the ball is pushed back to a player behind to create more space, set up a give-and-go or through pass, or switch the attack in another direction.

Bending the Ball — Putting a spin on the ball so it curves to the right or left in flight . . .and annoys keepers no end.

Blind Side — Area out of an opponent's field of view where a player can move to receive a pass. (Like quarterbacks, soccer players with good peripheral vision have a "leg" up.)

Caution — A "yellow card," shown a player for a serious infraction, warning him that another such foul will mean a "red card," and removal from the game. (With free substitutions, the coach may bench that player for a while rather than risk losing him, and having only ten players the rest of the game.)

Center Circle — The 10-yard circle around the middle spot on the field where play begins at the opening of each half or restarts after a goal. Opposing players have to remain beyond that circle until play begins.

Center Forward — The primary striker, the player in the middle of the forward line most responsible for scoring goals.

Center Fullback — The defender in the middle when there are only three fullbacks in all.
Center Spot — That point in the middle of the field where play begins at the opening of each half, and after a goal.
Centering Pass — Crossing the ball from a wing position into a potential scoring area in front of the goal.
Charging — A foul, resulting in a direct free-kick for the other team, incurred by colliding with or shoving an opponent other than when contesting side-by-side for the ball.
Clearing — Thwarting a dangerous attack by kicking the ball away without worrying too much where it ends up. This also applies to the goalkeeper punching, kicking, or throwing the ball out of the goal area.
Corner-Kick — A direct free-kick from a corner awarded the attacking team when the ball goes over the endline last touched by a defender.
Creating Space — Spreading and softening the defense, typically by lateral movement up front, and bringing a fullback into the attack as the "12th player."
Crossing Pass — Another phrase for Centering Pass.
Cutting Down The Angle — What a gutsy keeper accomplishes by coming out of the goal to confront an attacker on a breakaway, giving him a smaller target, and maybe forcing a hurried shot.
Dead Space — Areas occupied by players on the other team and therefore to be avoided when on the attack. (Dead space in caused by failure to create *live* space.)
"Direct" — Short form of free-kick awarded for major fouls from which a goal can be scored without anyone else touching the ball. (See "Indirect.")
Dribbling — The soccer equivalent of basketball, controlling and moving the ball with the feet.
Drop Ball — A restart by the referee similar to a face-off in hockey when a no-penalty situation . . .ie. injury or intrusion onto the field . . .causes an artificial break in the action.
Drop Kick — Harking back to the pre-placekick era of our football, when a keeper half-volleys rather than punts the ball to get off a lower, faster kick.
Ejection — Removal of a player from the game after a red card or two yellow card (caution) offenses. Their team plays short the rest of the game, and generally the player also sits out the next

game. (One reason soccer players learn to control themselves.)
Endline — Out-of-bounds line at opposite ends of the field, and including the goal line.
Far Post — The goal upright farther from the ball.
FIFA — Federation Internationale de Football Association, the governing body of world soccer headquartered in Switzerland.
First Touch — Kicking or passing the ball without stopping it, as in a wall pass or give-and-go.
Forward — A player in the front line, including inners, wings and strikers.
Free-Kick — An inclusive term for both "direct" and "indirect" resulting from a penalty.
Fullback — A player in the defense, including sweeper and stopper.
Give-And-Go — Like a wall pass, where two players combine to penetrate the defense, typically one with the ball "giving" a quick back pass to the other, and "going" ahead at speed to pursue a first-touch return pass . . .being mindful of the offside rule if it pertains.
Goal Box — The 6 by 20 yard area right in front of the goal from which goal kicks are taken.
Goal Kick — A free-kick from the goal box when the ball has gone over the endline last touched by an attacker. Opponents have to stay outside the penalty area, and it's technically an "indirect," not that it matters much.
Halfback — A player in the midfield acting as the link between defense and offense.
"Hands" — Short form for intentional use of hands (or arms) or, if not intentional, the referee feels that the offending team gains an advantage. The penalty is a direct free-kick.
High Kick — While not specified as such in Law 12, a kick close to an opponent's face may be considered a "dangerous play," and cause an indirect free-kick.
"Indirect" — Short form of free-kick awarded for minor fouls where a goal *cannot* be scored unless someone else touches the ball after the kick has been taken. (See "Direct.")
"Inners" — Right and left inside forwards working within the wings, essentially replacing the center forward as strikers in a four-attacker mode.
Instep — Anatomically, the arched medial portion of the foot which, when applied to kicking, simply means the *laces*.

Inswinger — A spinning kick that curves (bends) towards the goal, often aimed to sneak just inside an upright.
Keeper — Short for goalkeeper.
Kick-And-Run — A hard-running style of play characterized by long passes designed to create breakaway scoring opportunities. (And in cold weather climes to prevent blood from congealing?)
Kickoff — Really a misnomer for an indirect free-kick taken from the center spot to restart play at the beginning of each half, and after a goal.
Linesmen — The two officials who assist the referee by patrolling the touchline and endlines flagging out-of-bounds, offsides, and other fouls he might not see. (They also signal substitutions to the referee.)
Live Space — Obviously the opposite of dead space, this is open space available for mounting an attack which is created by drawing (decoying) opponents away.
"Major" — Short for a major foul incurring a *direct* free-kick. (It becomes a penalty kick if it happens in the penalty area.)
Marking — Guarding an opponent whether with the ball or away from the ball. Marking may be tight or loose depending on the circumstances.
Midfielder — A traditional . . .actually more descriptive . . .term for halfback.
"Minor" — Short for a minor foul incurring an indirect free-kick.
Movement Off The Ball — Actions by players not in possession of the ball to create live (open) space for a pass. When on defense, movement to eliminate the other team's live space so as to close down their attack and create a turnover.
Near Post — The goal upright nearer the ball.
Obstruction — Similar to downfield interference in football, when a player deliberately blocks an opponent from the ball rather than going for the ball himself. (A minor foul unless, in the referee's opinion, flagrant or dangerous.)
Offside — Being in a position of unfair advantage as detailed in Law 11 . . .and pages 57-64.
One Touch — Another way of saying "first touch."
"Outswinger" — The opposite of an inswinger, bending the ball away from a cluster of opponents into live space such as during a corner or crossing kick.
Overlapping Run — On attack, when a player behind the ball sprints ahead into live space . . .usually on the outside . . .to receive a

pass. (If a fullback, it's another "12th player" situation since he's momentarily unguarded.)
Penalty Area (Box) — That critical 18 x 44 yard area where the keeper can handle the ball, and where, as within the 20-yard line in football, most things good and bad eventually occur.
Penalty Kick — A direct free-kick from 12 yards in front of the goal caused by a major infraction by the defense within the penalty area. (Over 80% of the time a goal results.)
Penalty Spot — A blob of white stuff 12 yards from the goal where the penalty kick is taken. (Nobody else is allowed within the penalty area or penalty arc 10 yards from that spot until the kick is taken.)
Pitch — Euphemism for playing field, perhaps derived from the fact that soccer surfaces are seldom level.
"Positionless Soccer" — Call it whatever you want, this is the concept of total interchangeability among field players . . .a wide-open (probably inevitable) style of play that is already making traditional formations less relevant.
Red Card — What the referee waves in the face of a player to signal ejection from the game.
Referee — The field official in total command of the game, including keeping the time.
Restart — Getting play going again after a goal, penalty, out-of-bounds, or other pause in the action.
Save — Catch, block, punch, or deflect by the keeper that prevents a goal.
Scissor Kick — An aerialist form of a volley kick in which the legs function like scissor blades to snap the ball off the instep. (When used to drive the ball back over the head, if the performer avoids hitting himself in the face he lands flat on his back. A small price to pay for an unexpected goal.)
Set Play — A pre-arranged maneuver designed to make the most of a restart.
Settling The Ball — After trapping the ball, making sure you have it under control before trying to do something with it.
Shielding — As in basketball, a dribbler keeping the body between the ball and an opponent to retain control. (The only defense mechanism may be a slide tackle between or around the opponent's legs.)
Slide Tackle — Looking a lot like a steal of second base, a defender slides into the ball, and kicks it away from an attacker.

Square Pass — A lateral (sideways) pass usually to a teammate coming up from behind into live space.
Stacked Defense — Pulling most players back into their own half of the field to protect a lead, and/or cause opponents to make mistakes out of sheer frustration that can be converted into quick-thrust scoring opportunities.
Stopper — In effect the "advance fullback" . . .the defender ranging slightly ahead of other fullbacks to prevent threats from materializing. The player usually marks the main striker on the other team, and often becomes the first link in a counterattack.
Strength Up The Middle — Adapting a baseball phrase to mean structuring a soccer team with the best players in the corridor between the goal areas, where most significant action occurs.
Striker — Definitions vary, but most often meaning the main scoring threat(s) — center forward in a 4-3-3, and "inners" in a 4-2-4 and 4-4-2.
Sweeper — The defender closest to the goal responsible for sweeping away anything unfriendly that penetrates the defense. (This is the only field player likely to undertake more *lateral* than up-and-back movement.)
Tackle — The process of taking the ball away from an opponent whether by sliding, poking, blocking, or just taking advantage of a dribbling mistake.
Through Pass — A sudden pass beyond the defense that may give a forward a breakaway scoring opportunity.
Throw-In — The method of putting the ball back in play after it has gone out-of-bounds across the touchline.
Touchline — Sideline in "soccer-speak."
Transition — The process of shifting from offense to defense, and vice versa. Also shifting from one phase of attack or defense to another as play unfolds. Naturally, the faster and smoother the better.
Trapping — A general term for gaining control of a pass or kick in any of several different ways — with the head, chest, stomach, thigh, or foot.
Triangles — How two attacking players position themselves vis-à-vis an opponent to give the ball carrier the option to pass with minimal danger of the opponent intercepting it.
Upright — One of the vertical 8-foot posts of square cross-section that form the outer limits of the goal, and support the 8-yard crossbar

which is also of square cross-section. (Why square? . . .so a kick that *shouldn't* deflect into the goal *won't*.)
Volley Kick — Striking the ball while it's in the air, usually with the instep. It can be straight ahead, sidewinder style, or by a scissor kick.
Wall — A barrier of defenders set up 10 yards from where a free-kick is being taken within range of the goal.
Wall Pass — A fundamental "first-touch" (and triangle!) two-on-one tactic, where a player acts like a wall for his partner, deflecting his pass around and beyond the defender.
Weak Side — Basically, just the *other* side of the field away from the action, and, therefore, from clusters of opponents.
Wing — Most often referring to an outside forward, but it can be prefixed to midfielder or fullback to also mean an outside position.
World Cup — The ultimate goal for national teams, contested every four years since 1930 (except during war-affected years). Well over 100 nations compete within several geographic zones to become one of the 24 "finalists." Coming together in a host country, they play 52 games, first round-robin, and then single elimination. (The winner ends up playing 7 games.)
Yellow Card — What the referee waves in a player's face to warn them that any further foolishness of that kind will get them thrown out of the game. (See Caution, Red Card.)
Zone Coverage — A term we're familiar with, meaning rather than mark man-to-man, players cover areas of the field. (Most commonly seen in the form of a stacked defense.)